The Red Dragoon

The Red Dragoon
With the 7th Dragoon Guards in the
Cape of Good Hope Against the Boers
& the Kaffir Tribes During the
'War of the Axe' 1843-48

W. J. Adams

The Red Dragoon:With the 7th Dragoon Guards in the Cape of Good Hope Against the Boers & the Kaffir Tribes During the 'War of the Axe' 1843-48

Manuscript by W. J. Adams.Published in 1941 as part of *Private Buck Adams 7th (Princess Royal's) Dragoon Guards on the Eastern Frontier of the Cape of Good Hope 1843–1848*
W. J. Adams narrative editorially restored by Leonaur

Published by Leonaur Ltd

ISBN (10 digit):1-84677-057-2 (hardcover)
ISBN (13 digit): 978-1-84677-057-9 (hardcover)

ISBN (10 digit):1-84677-043-2 (softcover)
ISBN (13 digit):978-1-84677-043-2 (softcover)

http://www.leonaur.com

Publishers Notes

In the interests of authenticity, the spellings, grammar and place names used in this book have been retained from the original edition.

The opinions of the author represent a view of events in which he was a participant related from his own perspective;
as such the text is relevant as an historical document.

The views expressed in this book are not necessarily those of the publisher.

Contents

"As soon as they caught sight of us they raised the cry "Rooi Badjies - Red Coats - and away they went as fast as their legs would carry them."

Buck Adams
7th Dragoon Guards

Chapter One
I Enlist in the Cavalry

I was born in the parish of Spitalfields,London.My father was a turner and I have no doubt had he been more attentive to his business I should never have been a soldier. Up to the time of which I am writing, I do not think I had ever seen half a dozen of soldiers at one time in my life.

However, in the month of March, 1843, our trade was in a very depressed state and I made up my mind I would go out and seek for a situation. I heard of one being vacant at Messrs. Morrison, Dillon & Co. of Fore Street, City, for which I applied, but was too late, after which I strolled westward.When near Charing Cross I saw a lad run over by a horse and cart. I ran into the road and picked the lad up and gave him over to a policeman to be taken to the hospital, when I observed a soldier standing by my side. He spoke of the accident, after which he said to me:—

"Do you feel disposed to join the Army?"

I answered instantly and without one moments hesitation, "Yes, I do."

He placed in my hand a shilling which he appeared to have had quite ready for the purpose, then informed me that I had enlisted in Her Majesty's 15th Hussars, who were then stationed in India but would very shortly be returning to England.

By this time I found myself in front of the bar of a public house whither I had been led by the Sergeant, who proposed that we should "Do a brandy and soda." However, I had a glass of ale. For our refreshment I tendered the shilling which I had received from the Sergeant. I received no change. Another man was standing at the bar whom I heard say:

"Foolish young fellow; sold a life's liberty for a glass of ale."

After this I was taken to the rendezvous, The Hampshire Hog, Charles Street, Westminster, and was at once introduced to the landlord, Mr. Fox. A more lowbred, cunning, dissipated-looking man I never saw. I was also introduced to several Recruiting Sergeants. Sundry drinks were on the point of being ordered when some other men made their appearance, and I was taken upstairs, placed under the standard, found tall enough—5 ft. 7 inches—and right also as to chest measurement.

When we came downstairs again I observed my Sergeant, as I shall call him, in close conversation with another Sergeant, and I could see that I was the object of their conversation. I was asked if I would go into the 7th Dragoon Guards instead of the 15th Hussars, the former Regiment being under orders for The Cape of Good Hope—"The Garden of Eden," they said.

Thinking I should like to go abroad in preference to being a soldier at home, I consented and was accordingly handed over to my new master; and at the same time was introduced to a respectable looking young man who on the previous day had enlisted in the same Regiment. We were informed by the Sergeant that we could go where we pleased, but must be present the following morning at 10 o'clock to receive our pay and orders as to our future movements.

Each of us having a little money, we went out together for the remainder of the day. We visited Millbank Prison, my companion having a relative who was one of the officials at that institution. When my companion told his relative that he had enlisted for a soldier, the latter replied:

"We have plenty of soldiers here undergoing various terms of imprisonment, and I am of opinion, by what I know of your stubborn, self-willed disposition, that it will not be long before you are again a visitor here, and then very much against your inclination."

The conversation my companion had with his relative did not appear to increase his liking for the Army, as on our journey back to the rendezvous, he suddenly stopped and said he had made up his mind not to go for a soldier but should go to his relations in the country. We parted and I never saw him again.

On reaching the rendezvous and having ascertained that I could have a bed there, I decided to remain for the night. I was shown into a room where there were five or six small bedsteads. I was informed by the servant—a most repulsive-looking woman— that I could take which bed I pleased. Had I had the most remote idea of the misery of that night, I should have preferred to walk the streets rather than have entered that bedroom—the most vile and filthy den in which I ever put foot.

The next morning I was taken before the Inspecting Surgeon and examined.He said I was very slight for a Heavy Dragoon, and asked if I would go into a foot Regiment instead of Cavalry. I said I would be a horse soldier or none at all.At length he passed me as fit for a "Heavy Dragoon."

In due time I was taken before a Magistrate and sworn in, after which I received ten shillings. I then told the Sergeant that I should go and bid my parents and friends good-bye, when he informed me that I must go back with him to the rendezvous first as there were some trifling things to be settled there.

I said I was not aware of anything I had to settle as I had received nothing at the house except a night's lodging and breakfast the following morning, for both of which I had paid the landlady, Mrs. Fox, and had no recollection of having had anything what ever in the house beside what I had already paid for.

When we reached the house, to my surprise, I was informed by Mr. Fox that I was indebted to him in the sum of nine shillings and eleven pence for refreshments supplied by my orders to the various Recruiting Sergeants.

Being perfectly satisfied that I had never given any such orders, I refused to pay the amount. the Sergeant was called upon as witness that I had at various times called for drinks, cigars, etc.,for which I had not paid. In vain I pleaded to the Sergeant, who said he must speak the truth. I had called for drink several times in his presence and had not paid for it. A dozen Sergeants might have been found who would have sworn to the truth of the landlord's statement. I was threatened with all sorts of punishment short of being shot. At length the ten shillings came from my pocket, and in return I received one penny in change. I learned afterward that I was not the only one by some thousands who had been swindled in a similar manner, as the house had been used for many years as a rendezvous for recruiting parties.

In a few days after, I was sent with a number of others to join our Regiment, which was then at Gosport awaiting embarkation. Our party consisted of about ten, among which there were two clerks both of whom had lost their character and one young gentleman who wore glasses,whose father was the reputed owner of several steamboats running between London and Margate. Everyone seemed to pity him,he seemed so very simple. In short in voice and manner he was more like a young girl, which caused him to be named by one of the party "Susan," and by that name he was known for many years after.

We had also two young gentlemen who had held good positions in a City Firm, but the said Firm being rather too slow for the fast notions of the gentlemen in question, they made up their minds to have a spree and then together enlist, which they did.One of our party was a tramp who had been enlisted in a Police Court by special authority; and, lastly, we had one young gentleman of our party who had enlisted the day after he came out of the House of Correction, where he had been luxuriating for the past twelve months.

In due course we arrived safely at Gosport, and were taken at once to the Barracks. On our journey from the railway I walked by the side of "Susan." The rain came down very heavily. Poor fellow, I saw tears in his eyes several times. None of us had broken our fast that day; we were wet through, cold and hungry. As far as I was personally concerned, I thought it was a very rough beginning.

When we reached the Barracks we were placed in front of the office door. A few kindly words were spoken by the Colonel from the shelter of the passage, and we were drafted off to the various Troops to which we had been appointed. Myself and "Susan" were both sent to the same Troop.

On reaching the Barrack room, we found the Troop were just sitting down to dinner. I was at once taken possession of by a huge Irishman who stood 6 ft.$^1/_2$ inches high, not a particle of the upper part of whose face was discernible for the amount of hair which covered it. He placed me at the table and before me a plate of boiled meat, a basin of soup and a piece of bread. Potatoes with their jackets on came rolling towards my plate from both ends of the table, each man contributing one or two from his allowance. By the time they had finished their contributions I had a pile of potatoes in front of my plate, I should think about forty in number. Then I was questioned.

"Where do you come from, youngster? Who 'listed you?"

Then I heard my tall friend with the hairy face say:"Be jabers, he's not the size of a midge. Never want a horse to mount him so long as yez can get a buck goat."

"Now, my lad, don't be shy; take the jacket off yer taters,"said another. "Paddy, chuck down that lump of salt. Here's some pepper" —handing me some black-looking stuff in a piece of dirty paper.

At length, having satisfied my hunger, my long friend again came to me, and, taking a short black pipe from his mouth and drawing the stem through his hand, handed the pipe to me, saying:

"Yez will be able to get half a dozen draws out of it. It is all the bacca I've got until the pay comes out. Have yez got any money?"

Some of them then offered to show me the way to the canteen and as they were kind enough to give me part of their dinner, I could not well do less than give them some beer and tobacco in return. The quantity of beer and tobacco consumed in less than 10 minutes amounted to two shillings and sixpence, which I thought quite enough for what I had of them, and there I left them.

I shall never forget my first night in the Barrack room which was occupied by 25 single men, and 3 married men with their wives and families. Each family occupied one corner of the room, which was hidden from the rest, at night time only, by a sheet fastened across the corner. The scenes I witnessed and the language I heard on this, my first night in the Barrack room, I have never forgotten.

I was informed by the Corporal in charge of the room that, as there had been no time to get me my regular bedding, I must do the best I could with the one spare bed in the room, which was next the door, for this night at least. The "spare bed" (was) a dirty bag about six feet in length and two in breadth, containing a very small portion of straw which could not by any amount of ingenuity be made sufficient to cover the whole bottom of the very irregular iron bedstead, two blankets very old and thin, and an article termed in the Barracks regulations a rug.

After I had made several ineffectual attempts to get the bed to assume somewhat the appearance of an article of furniture of that name, I gave it up as entirely hopeless. I sat down on the bedstead, and began to consider what I had best do, when my long friend with the hairy face came to the rescue.

"What are yez sitting there for? Git up and make your bed; the lights'll be out prisintly. Yez haven't got yer mother to make yer bed for yer now, so don't be acting the stucorn. Yez had better wrap the blankets round yer. Being near the door, yez won't find it any too warm."

I thanked him for his kindness, when he said:"Have yez got any bacca?" But as I did not at that time indulge in the fragrant weed, I could not give him any.

There was a great noise in the room and as far as I could understand everyone appeared to be in an angry mood, when suddenly I heard a voice.

"Now, then, into bed. Lights out!"

The candle nearest to me was put out by a boot being thrown at it. For a few minutes all was quiet, then the noise was worse than ever, followed by a fight between a Roman Catholic and a Protestant, both Irishmen. The fight appeared to me to extend to a number of men on each side of the room. Being dark, I could not see how many were engaged in the melee. Iron candlesticks, plates, basins and other articles were thrown from one end of the room to the other. I was glad to creep beneath the blankets for fear I should fall in for a share of the missiles which flew about so plentifully.

The fight had lasted some time when suddenly all was quiet. Lights were brought into the room, when I saw a number of men come in with carbines in their hands. Then I heard several names called out. These men were ordered to dress themselves, and eventually were taken to the Guardhouse.

Sleep that night I could not. My long friend was right; I did not find it any too warm. With men coming in and going out, the door was open nearly the whole of the night. Glad indeed I was when I heard for the first time the Reveille which enabled me to rise. Shortly afterward "Susan" came to me. He had been less fortunate than I had. He had got a large bruise on the side of his head, caused by the heel of a boot that had been thrown at him by someone.

During the day all the recruits were ordered to attend the Regimental Office for the inspection of the Commanding Officer, who questioned several as to their age and other matters. He very nearly frightened poor "Susan" out of his senses when he addressed him:

"What's the matter with your head, sir? Drunk and fighting or fell down, which was it? Such conduct will not do in my Regiment, mind that!" "Susan" trembled from head to foot while the Colonel was speaking to him.

Having finished his inspection, the Colonel said he had that morning received two letters—which he held in his hand—in reference to two of our number. He said he wished us all to understand that it was of no consequence to him in what manner any of us had been brought up; all men on joining his Regiment were on terms of equality. Our future conduct alone would cause distinction, if any, hereafter. 24 years experience has convinced me how far, in many cases, the "future conduct" will affect the distinction in question.

In the afternoon I received a remittance from home, and my long friend proffered his services to show me where I could get it cashed, which offer I accepted. Having got the money, we then went to Southsea, and at night to a music hall. Several times I asked my companion if we had not better return to Barracks. He said as the Regiment was going on Foreign Service, any man was at liberty to take a few days' leave if he felt disposed to do so, in proof of which he directed my attention to a number of soldiers who were sitting in the same hall. Accordingly, we remained at Southsea until the following evening, when I made up my mind to leave my companion and return to Gosport.

On reaching the Barracks I was questioned by the Sergeant of the Guard as to my name, the Troop I belonged to and how long I had been away from Barracks. Looking at me very hard, he asked if I had not made a mistake and given him the wrong name. As I learnt afterwards it was a common occurrence for recruits to enlist in an assumed name.

However, after some conversation between the Sergeant and others, and again looking over the list of absentees, he said my name was not on the list, and that it was the fault of the Orderly Sergeant, who had called the roll the previous night at watch setting and had neglected to report my absence. He told me to go to my Troop room, and not on any account was I to say that I had been away from Barracks so many hours. The fact was that one half of the Regiment was drunk and the other half had all their work to do to maintain some little amount of discipline.

As there were a considerable number of married soldiers in the Regiment in excess of what was allowed by the "Regulations" to accompany their husbands on Foreign Service, the wives of all the Non-Commissioned Officers and Privates had to draw lots. Those who were successful would accompany their husbands; those who were not must remain behind as not one beyond the number allowed by the Regulations could go with the Regiment. If I remember right, it was only 5 women to each Troop of 54 men of all ranks.

The women who were unsuccessful were to be sent with their children to any part of the United Kingdom they chose to go to at the Government expense. Some of them, poor creatures, with a host of children and not a friend in the world, would have to go into the Workhouse. A subscription was made throughout the Regiment for them, and I believe everyone gave as far as his means would allow and not a few beyond it. The scenes at parting—husbands from wives and fathers from children—were such as I hope never to see again and a disgrace to the name of England.

One morning "Susan" came to me in a terrible state of mind. He said he had just been served out with his Regimental necessaries, and, after taking the whole of his bounty and Cavalry equipment allowance, his account book showed him to be one pound eighteen shillings and ninepence in debt. All he had received since the day he enlisted was two shillings and sixpence on passing the medical inspection, ten shillings on being sworn in, one shilling per day in London and only one penny per day since he arrived in Gosport.

We were told by the Recruiting Sergeant that we should only be allowed to draw a portion of our bounty as part of it would be required to pay for our Regimental necessaries; but we found out, as thousands had done before and since—

if all Cavalry Regiments were alike—that the bounty and Cavalry equipment allowance put together would not meet the cost by nearly two pounds. The consequence was the recruit was put under stoppages, and would receive only one penny per day until the amount owing was paid off. If the recruit was careful of his necessaries he might be clear of debt in six months; if otherwise, he would be years without receiving more than one penny per day. I have it on record of a well-conducted man who eventually attained to the rank of Troop Sergeant Major, being for four years after he enlisted—as a Private and Corporal —on one penny per day. I will admit that his was certainly an exceptional case.

Again (regarding) the quality and price of the articles supplied to the soldier; I have before me in my possession this minute a towel which was issued to me bearing, date 1st April, 1843. It measures in length 16 inches in width 12 inches. Quality, the very commonest description. Price charged,one shilling and a halfpenny;actual value at the date of issue, one penny and a halfpenny. Any soldier found in possession of an article not strictly regimental was guilty of Disobedience of Orders"—the greatest crime a soldier could be guilty of and one that would render him liable to such punishment as a Court Martial was competent to award.

Chapter Two
The Regiment Embarks for Africa

April 5th, 1843. The Regiment embarked on board Her Majesty's good ship *Rodney*, 92 guns. There were also four Companies of Infantry, a Battery of Artillery, besides women and children. The total number on board exceeded one thousand. Every man was supplied with a hammock cloth, lashings and two blankets. Each hammock was numbered, and a corresponding number was to be found at the place where the hammock should be slung.

I managed to sling my hammock, but in such a manner that I could not get into it, and I was not the only one. At last I gave it up as impossible and laid me down on the deck. During the night I awoke struggling to turn myself round, when I found I was being held fast to the deck. The flannel drawers I was wearing had made fast friends with the seams in the deck, which had only been newly pitched few days before we came on board.

All hands were piped up at 5 a.m. Hammocks neatly rolled and stowed away in the nettings by 5.30; then scrub, wash and holystone decks until 8; after which, breakfast. This and the four following days were taken up in stowing away the stores and getting ready for sea.

April 10th. Sailed from Spithead, and by this time I had mastered the difficulty of sleeping in a hammock. The fact was when I put it up the first night I had not put the lines in regular; but, having made a kind of chum with one of the sailors, he gave me the necessary instructions.

A few days after we had left Spithead I first witnessed flogging in the Service. Two sailors received four dozen lashes for being drunk on board the day before. One of them was quite a young fellow. He appeared to suffer the greatest punishment. Before the flogging was over I became insensible, and when I recovered I found myself in the sick bay. I was only too glad to get away and as by this time the flogging was over I went on deck again.

I expect must have looked somewhat pale, as everyone appeared to look at me very hard. One man said:"You must be a chicken-hearted fellow."

Another said: "Poor little fellow, he's not much bigger than a good buck rat."

Then again: "You will get the better of that babyism before you put in your 28 years."

But I may here remark once and for all that I never got rid of that horrible dread of witnessing a man being flogged. In vain I struggled and fought against it, but to no purpose. I have closed my eyes in order that I might not see the horrible brutality, but I could not shut out from my ears the sound of the"cat"each time it came in contact with the poor wretch's back. Several times on the field and in the temporary hospitals I have assisted in holding men undergoing amputation of leg or arm and other surgical operations, but never experienced the dreadful sensation which I have described on seeing a man flogged.

Whether from bad management or neglect of the authorities I know not—but most certainly it was the duty of the Commanding Officer to look after the rations of the men under his command—all Troops at that time embarking for Foreign Service were placed on what was termed "six upon four"— which signifies six soldiers on four seamen's rations,such ration consisting of pork and pea soup, beef and duff on alternate days. I can assert as a positive fact that on many occasions the allowance of meat has not exceeded two ounces. The allowance of biscuit should have been seven ounces, but I question very much if it ever exceeded half that quantity. A usual but rather laughable remark of the ship's cook was: "Well, sogers, good luck again to-day. Splendid soup; not a single pea broken." Those Messes whose turn it was to be served first would get what appeared to be a can of dirty water—I am sure it was more like that than pea soup. Those who were served last would get a can of peas hard as bullets.

Poor "Susan." Whenever I met him on deck the subject of his conversation was invariably on the nice things his mother made when he was at home and he used to say he was sure he should die of hunger before we reached the end of the voyage. As to my long friend with the hairy face, I was afraid to venture too near him as he always appeared so savagely hungry. How his enormous bulk was maintained on the "six upon four" scale, I could never imagine.

Three times each week we had a concert on deck— Monday, Wednesday and Friday, from 8 to 11 p.m.— and among such a number of men we could always manage to raise a pretty strong party for singing. The Officers would be seated in the boats which were stowed on deck, and the soldiers and sailors on the deck. If I were on board now, I should be asked to say sailors and soldiers, At all events I should be asked if I could not say one as well as the other. "Jack" never could bear the idea of soldiers being, put before sailors. At 9 o'clock a can of grog was given in charge of the Master of Ceremonies, who was invariably the Master-at-Arms; and each man, after singing a song, received a small tot of grog.

I had always been very fond of singing and at that time could repeat quite one hundred songs, besides recitations; yet it was some time before I could be persuaded to "come out of my shell," as the soldiers termed it. The tot of grog often induced men to make an attempt, but none were eligible for grog unless they could get through a moderate portion of a song. Some would be ordered by the Master-at-Arms to "Have another trial; it won't run grog for that bit."

Two days in each week, Monday and Thursday, were washing days—from 4 to 6 a.m. only—and done or undone, We were compelled to knock off the instant the bell struck or run the risk of the "taps," for there did not appear to me to be any punishment inflicted except flogging. The number of tubs for washing was about one for every forty men; therefore at least 38 of that number had to resort to other means for washing their clothes. It must be done some way or another. The order is given for washing, and it must be obeyed.

I must certainly admit that I found some difficulty for some little time, not having been accustomed to get up my own linen, but as I had from the beginning made up my mind to make the best of a bad job, I managed pretty well. No man was allowed to wash at any time except in the two hours of those days I have mentioned—unless he could do it unknown to the numerous Petty Officers who were invariably on the lookout, and appeared to derive a considerable amount of pleasure in detecting and reporting any of the soldiers for the slightest infringement of the rules, and more particularly a Marine. Sailors and they could never agree.

When I could not succeed in getting a tub, I used to endeavour to wash one or two articles when on watch from 8 to 12 p.m.—which hours fell to every man every third night. I would get a rope and fasten my clothes to the end of it, then creep over the bows of the ship, make fast the rope, and let them drag through the sea for 2 or 3 hours. This was against all orders, still I was fortunate in never being caught doing it. After the drag through the water I used to hold them up by the corners and let the wind blow through them until I went below at 12 o'clock, when I would spread them over the bottom of my hammock and lay upon them. When I arose at 5.30 a.m. I invariably found them sufficiently dry to put them on, and I do not remember that I ever caught a cold from so doing.

One night when I hauled in my line I found a "swab"— article used for cleaning the deck—attached to it instead of my clothes. This was a trick played upon me by one of the sailors. But he brought them to me the following day, and had washed them very nicely. Another time they got loose from the line and I lost them altogether; and once, when the sea was very rough, I hauled in my line and found that my clothes had been torn into shreds. But I had not been on board much over a month before I could do quite as well as most of the old hands. Sometimes (I) was obliged to display a little of my pugilistic ability when one of the old fellows would be trying to take my tub away from me before I was done washing and that simply because I was only a recruit. The whole of the Troops and Crew were divided into three watches, one of which was always on deck; and the watches were regulated so the hours on deck were changed every day. I soon became a great favourite with all on board. I was never absent from the singing party, whether it was my watch on deck or not; and I often came in for little extras in the shape of a plate of scraps from the cuddy—then to me a luxury—which many a dog would have turned from in disgust.

On Sunday all hands appeared in their best; the decks were made particularly clean;and all the ropes were tastefully coiled down which, unless in cases of emergency, were left that way until evening. We had Divine Service at 10.30 a.m. on deck when the weather permitted. I always looked upon Sunday as the most pleasant day of the week;not that we had any more to eat on that day, but there was sure to be no flogging going on on that day.

The Captain of the ship was seldom seen on deck except for Divine Service and to witness flogging. He appeared to derive very great pleasure from these exhibitions. There was only one time his voice was heard; at each stroke of the "cat", he would exclaim:"Bosun's Mate, do your duty, sir!" He was always of opinion that the Mates did not flog hard enough. He was a poor, feeble old man. If the day was very bright he took a walk on the quarter deck, leaning on the arm of the Chief Officer—but I must tell you that I have seen Officers in the Army in command of large numbers of men who were equally as feeble as the Captain of H. M. Good Ship *Rodney*.

The first port we reached was Madeira.Here we remained five days taking in stores and provisions. The "bumboats" came alongside daily, and all who had the means revelled in the luxuries of fried fish, bread, oranges, figs, plantains and many other things which I do not now remember. On the last day of our stay I laid in a stock of bread which I thought with economy would last me some time, as I appeared to suffer much from insufficiency of food. But I was not permitted to enjoy the luxury of "soft tack"for long.On the first night after leaving Madeira someone took a fancy to my bread and was not satisfied with a portion, but took the whole, bag and all.

The following morning a Corporal told me he had orders to take me on deck before the Captain of my Troop. One of the Petty Officers had reported having found some article belonging to me on the main deck. I guessed at once what the article was that had been found. My Captain said:

"What do you mean, sir, by leaving your things laying about the deck?"Then, addressing my Sergeant Major said: "Let him have three days punishment drill."

I endeavoured to explain to the Captain what had happened but was cut short with "Silence. It is an offence to leave your things kicking about."

The Serjeant Major explained that this was the first offence since I joined the Regiment so I was pardoned.

For breakfast each man received a pint of cocoa; and, for those who could drink it, I have no doubt it was very nourishing.But the very sight of it was enough for me;there seemed to me to be at least half an inch of black grease always floating on top of it.There were several like myself who could not drink it, therefore our breakfast consisted of about two ounces of biscuit and a drink of water.

Well indeed do I remember one day several men requested to see the Commanding Officer for the purpose of bringing to his notice the quantity and quality of the meat ration which had been supplied that day. I could safely swear that it did not exceed 11/2oz. and poor quality.

The Commanding Officer gave a smile as he passed and turning round sharply said "You get all that is allowed you by Her Majesty's Regulations and in my opinion you are abundantly and sumptuously fed." He then gave an order that the first man who made any complaint in reference to the food either in its quantity or quality was to be made a prisoner forthwith and that man should have the benefit of a Court Martial to test the validity of his complaint. As a matter of course there were no more complaints after that. But had there been anyone so foolish as to complain again, the result most probably would have been as follows. A Court Martial—General, District or Regimental— according to the complainant's—or should I say—prisoner's previous character, and the following would be the result:—

"The Court, having maturely weighed the evidence in support of the prosecution, together with what the prisoner has urged in his defence, is of opinion that the complaint of the prisoner is groundless, vexatious and subversive of good order and military discipline, and do hereby sentence prisoner number 0000 to undergo an imprisonment of 84 days with hard labour."

Such little affairs as these often prevented a great deal of trouble and vexation. I was never an advocate for frivolous complaints, and it was some time before I ventured to make one of any kind.

Within ten days there had been no less than six brutal exhibitions—five for insubordination and one for drunkenness. I always got away as far as possible from the spot where the punishment was being inflicted—that was no trouble, as all appeared to me to push as near as possible to the unfortunate wretch.

The next port we reached was Rio de Janeiro. Here we remained eight days, taking in provisions and fresh water. The bumboats furnished the usual harbour luxuries, but as I had invested all the cash I possessed in bread at Madeira, I had none to spend here. Each day several boats came round the ship containing Portuguese soldiers, who were always begging for tobacco or anything else we chose to give them. They appeared very poorly clad and badly paid. Many years later at Capo di Verde I had an opportunity of proving my conjecture to be correct.

A few days after we had left Rio, a young soldier was made a prisoner and placed in irons for stealing a forage cap, the property of a comrade. The simple facts of the case were these:

Some one had taken this man's cap from the place where he usually kept it. He saw another cap lying on the ground with the chinstrap partly torn off, and very naturally concluded that the owner of this one had taken his. Consequently he tore off the broken piece of strap, threw it out of the porthole, put the cap on his head and went on deck.

In the meantime a report had been made of a cap having been lost by a recruit. However the missing cap was found in his the young soldier's possession and he was charged with stealing it. The following day he was sentenced to receive four dozen lashes with the "thief's cat," which differs from the ordinary cat, each of the nine tails having nine knots in it and each knot would cut a hole in the flesh.

I never saw a man so badly punished as this man was. His back was like a lump of black jelly. After the punishment was inflicted, he was taken to the hospital. The Surgeon was heard to say that the man was more severely punished than he would have sanctioned. He was not the Surgeon who was present when the punishment was inflicted. Had he been on duty, I have no doubt he would have stood by with as much unconcern as did the one who witnessed the punishment. I never saw but one case during the whole of my 24 years service where the Surgeon interfered to stop further punishment.

About the middle of September we reached Table Bay, having been over five months making the passage. The day following our arrival a portion of the Regiment was drafted into *Nautilus*, an old transport, and ordered to Algoa Bay. The remainder of the Regiment disembarked at Cape Town for the purpose of taking horses up the country for the use of the Regiment. These had been purchased for us prior to our arrival.

When leaving Table Bay the Captain of the *Rodney* was on deck; still I am not going to say that his presence caused the accident which befell us. The two old tubs came into collision, the *Nautilus* carrying away the bowsprit and some gear attached to it of the great *Rodney*.

When I look back and think of the voyage, I wonder we ever reached our destination. 'Tis certain the Captain had little to do with it, as he was so very seldom on deck unless for Divine Service or to witness flogging. From the latter he was never absent. I never knew him to remit one lash of the number awarded. No matter whether the victim was old or young, he would insist on the whole of the punishment being inflicted.

Chapter Three
We Arrive at the Cape of Good Hope

We reached Algoa Bay on the fifth day and, having cast anchor, we soon began to disembark by means of surf boats, each boat taking about 10 men besides the darkies who were working the boats. Two of the soldiers' wives came in the same boat with me. We found the landing without getting a wetting somewhat difficult. The boat was run as high as possible up the beach. We then had to watch the receding wave, jump out and make a run for it or we should have been caught by the next wave before we could have got clear of it.

Several darkies were on the beach, and I then noticed for the first time that they were all quite naked, including those were working in the boat. They had not a particle of clothing on them. It was part of their work to carry invalids, women and children from the boat to the beach, but on account of their peculiar appearance the women at first declined their assistance, but on being informed that they must either be carried by these men or run through the water themselves, they at length consented, doing as the Irishman did, "shutting their eyes and looking another way."

When we had all landed we marched a short distance and eventually took up our quarters within the prison walls of Port Elizabeth, and each man received one pound of bread and a pint of wine. At whose expense this was I cannot say, but I know this, I thought it the greatest treat I ever had.

After a stay of a few days, and the necessary number of waggons, with 12 bullocks to each, having been procured for the conveyance of Regimental stores and baggage, we began our march up the country, our final destination not being as yet decided upon. After a journey of about 16 miles, we halted and began our preparations for food and shelter for the night. All duties were told off alphabetically. The roll was supposed to be gone through correctly from A to Z, but I had discovered long since that the men at the beginning of the roll performed a greater amount of duty than those occupying the latter part of it. My name beginning with the letter "A" made me, as a matter of course, first for every duty; consequently I was first for the duty of Troop cook.

My first job was to go to the Commissariat waggon, where I received several lumps of beef. I asked the Corporal what I was to do with it, when he replied:

"Do with it? Why, boil it of course and make some soup."

At all events I bundled the meat into the camp kettles with some water I had got from a stagnant pool, and started a fire under them.

When I had got this far, one of the old soldiers was sent to instruct me as I was only a recruit, but I found I had quite as much knowledge of field cooking as he had. However, after some considerable time boiling and the men being hungry, we decided to dish up. The meat had the appearance of pieces of thick leather very much shrivelled up, and the soup put me in mind of water that greasy dishes had been washed in. However, the Troop were moderately satisfied, so I suppose it was as good as they expected.

The most important part of the day's proceedings was the fixing up of the tents. Not one man of the Regiment could boast of the slightest knowledge in reference to the putting up securely those miserable field pests called "Bell Tents." The complement of men to each tent was 12, but by the time half of that number had got inside with all their useless and useful accoutrements—the former far in excess of the latter— the tent was full.

At night it began to rain, so we were obliged to creep in and double up the best way we could. We had barely settled down for the night when a heavy thunder storm came on. The rain came down in such a manner that I never saw before. The thunder was very heavy, the lightning most vivid. Suddenly a heavy gust of wind came, and down went the tent.

Many times I have laughed heartily at the thought of that night.

The cause of the accident was the breaking of the socket of the tent-pole. The pegs were all well driven down and the door had been well fastened up; thus we were prevented from getting out from under the canvas. Some fell to cursing and some laughing. At length some of us managed to get out and draw some of the pegs, which enabled the rest to get clear of the heap of belts, swords, pistols, carbines, callabashes, haversacks, helmets, and a host of other useless appendages with which the soldier was encumbered.

As the pole of the tent was broken, the latter was utterly useless. We could not put it up without a pole, so we were obliged to stand in the rain and wait for daylight. Shortly after we started again on the march.

Each waggon was drawn by from 10 to 12 bullocks yoked in couples. A small native boy, invariably a Hottentot who is called "Forelooper," runs in front of the leading bullocks which follow him in the direction they were wanted to go. Sometimes the bullocks will not go without a Forelooper.

This day I was one of the baggage guard and was in charge of the rear waggon, the Forelooper of which had been suddenly taken ill. The bullocks would not go on without some one in front of them, and it was equally necessary that the whip should be behind them. Under those circumstances there was the choice of two things—either to remain where we was until the Forelooper should be well enough to do his work, or for me to take the place of the sick Hottentot boy. In the first place it was impossible to say how long he might be ill; and in the second place it was not a very creditable occupation for a Heavy Dragoon. However, I accepted the latter and several times I found two pairs of horns in rather close proximity to me behind which was any thing but pleasant.

At length we reached the Camp about one hour before sunset, much to the amusement of all hands at the novel occupation I had been engaged in.

Having outspanned—that is, unyoked the oxen— the driver, a young Englishman with whom I had become very friendly on the road, gave me an iron kettle and told me to follow the oxen because they would be sure to find the water. And I was to bring a kettle full, but was to be sure and get the water before the oxen got into it or they would stir it up and it would be like mud. For my trouble, I was to sup with him. He would prepare the food while I was away for the water. We were to have fried beef and "mealie scons" —the latter is cakes made of coarse flour and boiled in sheep tail fat.

I walked a considerable distance before I came in sight of the "*vley*"—a small pool of stagnant water. The oxen were too smart for me. They rushed into the water and very soon converted it into a pool of mud. But water must be had, whether thick or thin. The kettle was filled and I prepared to return to the waggon, but I discovered that I had lost my way, not having taken the precaution to note the part of bush I came from.

The oxen did not appear to be in any hurry to return and I did not know in what direction to go. The shades of evening were coming on fast. I turned first one way, then another. The thought of spending a night in the bush, with visions of hungry lions staring at me with open mouths, was anything but pleasant.

Suddenly I heard a slight noise near the spot I was standing. On looking about me I caught sight of a large hyena feeding off the carcass of a goat. He made a move, and, I fancied, fixed his eyes on me in a most unpleasant manner, which caused huge drops of perspiration to run down my face. I knew not what to do or which way to run. I lifted the kettle above my head with the intention of throwing it at him should he attempt to attack me. It is needless for me to say that by this time I lost all my water from the kettle, but was most agreeably surprised to hear him give a bit of a growl, I suppose for my intrusion, and then walk off himself.

I certainly felt anything but comfortable. It was getting dark. Presently I heard the crack of a driver's whip, and the whole of the oxen moved in one direction. I followed them and they led me direct to the waggon. The oxen well understood the cracking of the whip was the calling of them to go to the waggon to be fastened up for the night.

I did not reach the Camp until two hours after sunset with the kettle but no water, and about a handful of mud, in it. I had also lost the lid of the kettle. I got any amount of abuse from my friend, the driver, and had to go to my Troop for my supper. It was a very long time before I ventured to go alone for water again by myself. This being my first adventure in the bush, I remember it very well.

At length we reached Graham's Town, which was then the largest and principal town on the Frontiers; and on the following day the Head Quarters of the Regiment were ordered to proceed on to Fort Beaufort, leaving one Troop at Graham's Town for the purpose of forwarding any horses that might arrive for the Regiment.

By some mistake me and "Susan" were left behind; we should have gone on with the other recruits with Head Quarters of the Regt. I had not as yet had but very little drill, and had not crossed a horse. In fact, I had not even got my uniform as I was still wearing the coat and vest I wore when I enlisted, with a pair of Regimental trousers. But in those days it took a great deal longer to make an efficient Dragoon than it does at the present time.

After a few days I succeeded in borrowing a suit of uniform; and, "Susan" having done the same, we determined to pay a visit to Graham's Town as "Susan" was about writing a long letter to his mother and was anxious to gain as much information as possible for that purpose.

The first information we received was that the inhabitants were nearly all discharged soldiers, emigrants or liberated convicts from Robin's Island, and the remnants of the Royal South African Corps. Our informant was a black member of the Cape Mounted Rifles. His name was Sergeant Japps, and I believe the ugliest nigger I ever saw. He said:"Ah, Johnny, plenty white people here, great rogues."

There is no mistake but he done his best to convince us that a great many of them went to Church on Sunday, but that they studied hard all the rest of the week how each could most effectually rob his neighbour.

In the course of our ramble we passed by the Garrison Office. An Officer was standing at the door who after looking at us very hard for some little time, called to us and asked what Regiment we belonged to and whether anyone inspected us before we left the Barracks, and concluded by saying:

"Two such objects in soldiers' uniform I never saw."

If there was any conceit in either of us previous to this, I should think what we had just heard was quite enough to take it out of us. The Officer ordered us to wait for a few minutes. We did so. At length he came out accompanied by the Garrison Sergeant Major, and said:

"Take these two men with this note to the Officer commanding the Troop of the 7th Dragoon Guards with my compliments."

On our way back the Sergeant Major told me that I had a jacket on large enough for two of my size, and that "Susan" had come out with a nightcap on his head instead of a forage cap. When we reached the Barracks the Captain gave an order that we were not to be allowed outside the gates any more. A few days after the above affair me and "Susan" were ordered to be sent to Fort Beaufort with two others; one an ex-Troop Sergeant Major, the other, ex-Sergeant. They had both been reduced to the ranks during the past week for drunkenness

The first day we reached Fort Brown, 24 miles— not a

bad day's march for a recruit. A few sappers were stationed at the Fort who were about building a bridge across The Koonap River. These men treated us very kindly. The following morning we continued our journey and reached Fort Beaufort in the evening, having done 46 miles in the two days.

Christmas Day, 1843. I have a faint recollection of being one of a number of men sitting in a kind of shed round a camp kettle and a large tin dish; the former containing beef and soup, the latter a large plum pudding. We had no other place to take our meals as the Barracks was undergoing the process of fumigation on account of the disease of ophthalmia having broke out to a considerable extent among the Troops.

In January, 1844, the disease became so bad that more than one-third of the Regiment was in the Hospital. I was there 12 weeks myself, a considerable portion of which time I was blind with both eyes. We had medical men from India, St. Helena and other places, but they could not master the disease. At length it was decided to send the whole Regiment into Camp on the banks of the Kat river, where, after a short stay, the disease left us. But a considerable number of men had to be discharged.

In reference to the cause of the disease; there were not two medical men of the same opinion. I will give mine and let the world judge for itself.

1st. 100 men crowded into a space not sufficiently large to accommodate half that number.

2nd. Rooms very badly ventilated and not sufficient light.

3rd. No utensils or accommodation of any kind for ablution, the barrack slop pail being the only article available, and that was the usual receptacle for all kinds of filth.

4th. Scarcity of water. I have seen from 15 to 20 men in succession trying to wash their flesh in less than half a gallon of water which had the appearance of *Rodney* pea soup.

5th and lastly. The stables for the horses were situated half a mile from the men's Barracks, and this distance had to be traversed at the very least ten times every day. The sun at this time of the year was very hot at midday. Each Troop consisted of 54 men of all ranks and 45 horses; and if 40 men out of 54, less the Troop Sergeant Major and Sergeants, were away from their horses on duty or working as tailors, shoemakers, saddlers, farriers, saddle-tree makers, Officers' servants, Officers' Mess ditto and Hospital ditto and in short several other dittoes, the remaining 14 men would have to look after and clean the whole 45 horses.

I cannot say for certain but I am really of opinion that what I have stated would go a great way in the present age of common sense to account for the cause of the disease. A plentiful supply of water from the river soon removed the cause. But all this was in the last days of the "dark ages" of the Army— those "Good Old Days" that are still so tenaciously clung to by some of the old fogies.

Chapter Four

Spider

In due course I was dismissed from Recruit drill and returned as fit for field service. The Regiment had got its full complement of horses, but everyone admitted that they were much harder to break in than English horses. They were such terrible brutes for kicking. None of them were shod on the hind feet. Several men had good reason to remember the one that fell to my lot. When he could not get me off his back by plunging and kicking, he would throw himself down and try to roll over me.

Every evening the horses were ridden bareback to water, a distance of little over half a mile. Going, my beautiful charger, Spider, always went very quietly; but the moment he left the water he began his pranks, and for a long time he invariably left me on the ground and to walk to the stables. Some of the old soldiers who had steady horses used to say,

"If he can't ride that thing of a horse, why don't they get him a buck goat? That would be big enough for him." Although I was 5 feet 7 $\frac{1}{2}$ inches in height and my weight 10 stone 6 pounds, I was the shortest and lightest man in the Regiment.

One evening one of the old soldiers, who had paid sundry visits to the wine shed during the day, asked the Sergeant Major to let him "ride that goat of Adams's to water," and me to ride his horse.

"Yes," said the Sergeant Major. "Do so, O'Neill. See what you can do with the brute."

I was only too pleased at the chance of getting out of a fall. I had my eye on Spider. I saw Paddy pulling him about on his way to the water. I thought to myself, "Wait a bit."

We were all leaving the river when Spider began his

tricks. Paddy struck him with his fist between the ears, to do which he leaned somewhat forward. That was Spider's opportunity and he embraced it. He gave one or two buck leaps and a kick, and Paddy was sprawling on the ground, and Spider, as usual, cantering off to the stables.

The Riding Master by chance happened to witness this little bit of performance, and he asked the Sergeant Major how it was that I was not riding my own horse. The Sergeant Major explained, when the former said:

"Sergeant Major, mind that O'Neill attends extra riding drill until further orders; I never saw more slovenly riding in my life."

Thus Paddy got in for a considerable amount of extra riding through proffering to ride the "goat," as he called it.

At length me and Spider became better friends. The tumbles he gave me were less frequent, and fortunately I was never much hurt.

It would have been a good job if I could have said the same by others. Within one month there were two men in Hospital, each with a broken leg caused by my beautiful charger Spider kicking them while I was on his back at field drill. In the stable he was most vicious—bite and kick at everyone who came near him except me. I could do anything with him. He always fared very badly when I was away from him 24 hours on duty. Very few would venture any nearer to him than they were obliged. Whoever had the care of him at these times would merely throw some food to him taking good care not to venture too near.

One night a report reached the Fort that the Kaffirs had attacked Tumie Post, a small fort about seven miles from Fort Beaufort and near the Amatola Mountains. The Garrison alarm was sounded and one Squadron of Dragoons was ordered to saddle up at once and about midnight we started. It was not thought necessary to engage a guide. Certainly not. Everyone knew the way to Tumie; some had been there several times.

However, after riding about two hours it was quite

evident that not one of the Squadron knew where we were going. We had got into a thick bush, where we had to flounder about until daybreak, when we found we had been circling round very nicely so as to bring us within one mile of the place we originally started from three hours previous.

Half an hour's ride now brought us to the "beleagured" Fort. We nearly frightened the life out of the few people who lived there and the six soldiers who were stationed in the little stone tower which was called "The Fort." We very soon ascertained that the report was false, and we returned to Fort Beaufort.

It was rumoured the following day that the reported attack on Tumie Post originated in the Officer's Mess for a bit of a lark. Whether or not such was the case, I cannot say.

About the latter end of July, 1844, our Fort was visited by Makomo, one of the Chiefs of the Gaika tribe. He was accompanied by 27 women, his wives, and about 40 of his Chief Warriors, rain and thunder makers, witch finders, etc. He came to the fort for money which he was periodically allowed by the Government as compensation for a portion of land which had been appropriated by the British and which formerly belonged to the Kaffirs.

On these occasions Makomo always went to a *negotie winkel* (a kind of store) and purchased a new red nightcap in which he received the money. Whether it was his mode of measuring or counting the money, I cannot say. However, having got it, he and his followers proceeded to a wine shed and squatted on their haunches outside—Makomo in the centre; his favourite wife, a very young girl, by his side; the remainder of the ladies in a circle; and the gentlemen anywhere, but all striving to get as near the centre as possible.

About 20 bottles of the cheapest wine and about 6 bottles of "Cape Smoke"- a spirit distilled from peaches - were then brought out and placed on the ground near to the Chief. Having taken a draught from one of the bottles of Cape Smoke, he ejected a portion from his mouth into that of his favourite wife and this I saw repeated several times. After this part of the ceremony was over, there appeared a regular scramble for the bottles of wine. The Cape Smoke was reserved for the Chief and his wives. As the wine began to warm them they made a most horrible noise, shrieking like mad people for more of the *banya mooi umleela manza*—very nice firewater.

One of the ladies got drunk and was immediately carried to the river side, about 100 yards distant. Two Kaffirs got into the water and two remained on the bank, then they amused themselves by throwing the drunken woman from the bank into the river until she became sufficiently sober to walk without assistance.

Always when Makomo visited the Fort—why called a "Fort" I could never imagine, as there was not the least attempt at any kind of fortifications whatever, a number of infantry were always held in readiness to see them beyond the Boundary at sunset; and very often the soldiers would have the distinguished honour of carrying or assisting to carry some of the ladies, who were unable to walk, over the Boundary - a distance of about three-quarters of a mile.

I believe there had been times when the whole of them had been drunk long before sunset. Makomo, the Chief was always first to get drunk, and the rest very soon followed suit. The conduct of the Kaffirs on these occasions was disgusting in the extreme. They were allowed to go where they pleased utterly nude and the women not much better. I thought it very sad as they were a very fine race of people.

It was about this time that me and my comrade obtained leave for the day for the purpose of fishing in the Kat River. After we had been some time angling without a bite, we made up our mind to go on a voyage of discovery through the bush.

First we came to a Kraal - cattle enclosure. There were several huts with men, women and children. They began begging for tobacco, and before they had done with us they had got all the tobacco we possessed. I must admit that, in return, they gave us each a basket of milk.

Shortly after leaving the kraal we came in sight of what appeared to be a deserted hut. Yet we thought it somewhat strange that this hut should be so isolated and no kraal near it. However we made our way towards it and when within a short distance of it we heard a noise, and about 200 birds, very small, flew out from under what then appeared like a large umbrella but was in reality a bird's nest. There were a great number of nests beneath one roof. We retired a short distance, and the whole of the birds came back again and were very tame indeed. Five or six Kaffirs who had been following us would not allow us to touch the nest.

During our ramble we collected a number of birds eggs and captured a pair of birds about the size of an English blackbird with very beautiful plumage. At length, getting somewhat tired, we prepared to return to the Fort, and shortly afterwards I noticed that the number of Kaffirs who were following us had increased to over a dozen. Several times they came quite close to us, which made me feel anything but comfortable. I told my companion that I could see plain enough that they intended to molest us in some way or another. One of them carried a long *rhiem*—strip of hide—in his hand and kept swinging it about in a very peculiar manner.

We had walked some considerable distance and were delighted when we came in sight of the Fort. Me and my companion were walking side by side with the Kaffirs close by. Suddenly the *rhiem* was thrown over us. We were thrown to the ground and fastened together, my right arm to my companion's left. We were then loosened just sufficient to enable us to walk, and they made us understand they were going to take us to the Fort.

On nearing the fort several men of the Regiment saw us and were going to rescue us from the Kaffirs. Fortunately, some person came up who could partially understand the Kaffir language, and informed us that we had done something wrong and the Kaffirs intended taking us to the

Garrison Office. All the Regiment turned out and had a hearty laugh at the position we were in—tied together and surrounded by a dozen naked Kaffirs.

On reaching the Office we were again laughed at by the Officers who were present. The affair being investigated through the interpreter, it appeared that some time back an order had been given in the Garrison that no soldier was to go beyond the British Boundary, and the Kaffirs were also instructed at the same time that they would receive a reward of ten shillings for every soldier they found in Kaffirland and brought to the Garrison Office. These orders were given in order to prevent deserters passing through Kaffirland to enable them to reach the Dutch Settlements beyond the Orange River. Me and my companion were ordered to pay the reward—ten shillings.

Here I ventured on my first complaint. I told the Adjutant that I had never heard of any such order being given and I objected to paying the ten shillings, and wished to see the Commanding Officer in order that I might lay my complaint before him. But I was cut short by the Adjutant saying sharply:

"Silence, Sir! Do as you are ordered. Pay the ten shillings and make your complaint afterwards."

As I was not at the moment in possession of ten shillings, my Sergeant Major was directed to advance that amount and I was to be placed under stoppages until it was repaid. As it happened, the Sergeant Major had not sufficient cash about him to pay the ten shillings for each of us, and some little delay was caused in procuring the amount.

In the meantime the Commanding Officer made his appearance and some conversation took place between that gentleman and the Adjutant, and both adjourned to the Regimental Office. During their temporary absence the Kaffirs kept very close to us. At length the two Officers came out. They had made the discovery that the order was issued prior to our Regiment arriving in the Colony and had never been promulgated to the Regiment, consequently the fine of ten shillings was remitted, much to the disgust of the Kaffirs. But the Commanding Officer made each of the leaders a present of half a crown, and in the course of the day the order was made known to the Regiment.

It was only a few days after this little affair took place when a young Officer, being under the impression that the above order did not apply to Officers, but was merely intended to prevent Soldiers deserting, was taking a ride in Kaffirland a short distance beyond the Boundary when the Kaffirs came upon him and made him prisoner. They took the bridle from his horse and the stirrups from the saddle. They then tied his hands behind him and sent him about his business. They would not trouble themselves to take him to the Garrison Office as they were not certain whether they were right in stopping an Officer. I believe they done it out of revenge for not getting the reward for me and my comrade. The Officer in question — I will not give his name for he is still living made his way to the nearest habitation in the Fort and got his hands released, but not before he had been seen by some of the men of the Regiment. The following day Makomo sent in the bridle and stirrups, with an apology to the Officer for the conduct of some of his Tribe.

September, 1844. I was sent with a detachment consisting of 50 of the 7th Dragoon Guards, 4 Companies 91st Regiment and 150 Cape Mounted Rifles, to form a Camp of Observation on the Umdallah Heights.

On a portion of the ground where our Camp was pitched the grass was 12 feet high and interfered with the proper formation of the camp, besides being dangerous in such close proximity. The Officer Commanding the Infantry who wanted the ground for his men said:

"Oh, set fire to it."

One of the men suggested that the safest plan would be to cut it down and burn the stubble, as there might be some difficulty in putting the fire out when it got well hold of it. But the suggestion emanating from a Private Soldier was, as a matter of course, pooh poohed, and the grass was set on fire.

Very slight precautions were taken to prevent the fire going anywhere the wind might carry it. A few men were placed with branches of trees with orders to beat out the fire when it should reach a certain spot. But when the fire got well hold of the dry grass, most of which was half an inch in diameter, it drove all before it. The men with the branches had to beat a hasty retreat. Tongues of fire were carried by the wind, and five of the tents belonging to the men, with their contents, were destroyed. I believe the expense of this little freak fell on the Officer who gave the order.

There was certainly one most remarkable fact connected with this affair. Each of the tents destroyed contained the pouches belonging to the men who occupied them, and were fastened round the tent pole. Each pouch contained 60 rounds of ball cartridge. Although the tents were entirely destroyed and the men's clothing partly so, not a single round of the ammunition exploded. But the Infantry Soldier's pouch was a very different article to what it is at the present time.

I should like to compare the weight of his accoutrements these days with the huge knapsack, straps, heavy cross belts, Brown Bess, bayonet and bell-top "chaco" of 40 years ago. Again that implement of torture worn around the neck which was called a "stock." A more appropriate name could not be found for it—a broad band of leather hard as a board. No matter whether the man had a long or short neck, they were all cut to one uniform size, and the man was bound to wear it as issued to him from the Quartermaster's store and any man found reducing the size of his stock would have been severely punished.

Chapter Five
I Earn a Nickname

Another circumstance occurred while in this camp which proved fatal to one of the parties concerned. About 20 of us were employed cutting trees in the bush on the side of the hill about 150 yards from the Camp. Something took place between one of our men and a Kaffir woman who had come up from the valley to sell milk. They had been seen by some Kaffirs from the valley. The first intimation we received of the matter in question was seeing a number of Kaffirs running towards us. Within half an hour there were about 200 gathered around us and we could see them coming from all directions.

Our party, thinking it would be best to be on the safe side, returned to the Camp and fortunately we were not far from it. If we had been, there was one of our number who would never have reached it. No Kaffirs were allowed to enter our Camp or to come within a certain distance of the outer line of Sentries; still they came as near as possible.

By this time there were at least 500 collected; and the number continued to increase as the signal which had been given by the Kaffirs was forwarded from place to place. It is truly wonderful the immense distance the voice of a Kaffir may be heard in some parts of the bush. None of them were armed as they were not supposed at that time to be in possession of arms, yet in how short a time after (when the war started), every Kaffir was found in possession of a gun and plenty of ammunition.

However, they made a most terrible noise and continued to point to the man in question, he being conspicuous wearing a shirt of a peculiar colour to those around him. We could not understand what they said, but their actions were unmistakeable by which they gave us to understand that if they could only get hold of him, they would strangle him or cut him to pieces joint by joint.

As their number had by this time increased to about one thousand, the whole of the Troop in Camp were ordered to turn out under arms, after which the Kaffirs gradually dispersed. During the evening immense numbers were seen gathering in the valley, and double sentries were posted round the Camp. About midnight a very large fire was made in the valley. Some thousands of Kaffirs had assembled, when a woman was seen with a *rhiem* fastened round her body. And amidst the yells of the assembled multitude, she was dragged through and through the fire until she was burnt to death. The tumult continued until daylight the following morning.

Our Camp was very badly situated for water, every drop of which had to be carried up from the valley, a distance of nearly one mile. At length we dug large holes in the sides of the hill to catch the rain water, which answered very well for washing purposes.

One day myself and several others were washing and shaving at one of those holes when several Kaffirs came up and began dancing and begging for tobacco. One of them was watching me most intently. A small mirror I held in my hand appeared to attract his attention. When I held it to his face he shouted to the others, then looked behind it. I thought the fellow would have gone mad with astonishment. Several others gathered round and had a look at it. One of them appeared to be explaining to the others what the mirror really was, according to his idea. They continued looking at it for some time, first one and then another. At length I got it from them and, having finished my shave, I made an offer to shave one of the Kaffirs—the one who had been paying me so much attention, to which he willingly consented. The luxury of a good razor to them was unknown.

However I dipped a lump of soap in the water and began rubbing it into his beard, but was a considerable time before

I could raise a lather in consequence of the mass of grease and red clay with which his face was covered. At length I succeeded and began to operate on the phiz of my sable friend, who appeared to enjoy it very much, exclaiming repeatedly "*banya mooi*"—very nice—It was my intention to have left him with one side of his face unshaved, and I was about to leave him when he caught hold of me with one hand and kept passing the other over his face. I began to think I had done wrong in shaving the fellow, as his companions all gathered round me and were talking in a very excited manner—at least so I thought. At length they made me understand that they intended to keep me there until I had made the other side of his face as smooth as that which I had been operating upon.

By this time all the rest of my companions were gone and I was alone with about a dozen Kaffirs, each in possession of a *nobkerry*—a short stick with a large ball carved on the end, in which are inserted some kind of teeth. And another very unpleasant fact was that I was for duty that afternoon and felt satisfied that even then I was behind time.

However, as there was no getting away from them, I was obliged to commence operations on the other side of his face. He stood very patient while I was rubbing the soap into his beard, but when I put the razor to his face he was anything but patient. He jumped and screamed. The clay and sand had taken all the cut out of the razor. In vain I tried to finish my task. The fellow grinned in a most savage manner. I tried to sharpen the razor on the front of my boot. The more I scraped, the more he grinned. At length I was allowed to leave them, and the dirty face of my sable friend had spoiled the only razor I had in the world.

When I reached the Camp I found that I was two hours behind the time I should have paraded for duty. I had been reported absent and another man had been put on guard in my place. I was made a prisoner at once and my crime made out— "absent from guard mounting and not returning until two hours afterwards." This was sent to the Officer in Command of the Dragoons who was fortunately for me most favourably disposed towards me. I was ordered to be brought up at once.

My crime being read over to me, I was asked what I had to say in defence. I explained to the Officer fully all the particulars how I had been detained by the Kaffirs through foolishly attempting to shave one of them. Several times the Officer had to turn his face from me in order to restrain himself from an outburst of laughter. However I got off without punishment, but was told in future when I wanted to go as a barber among the Kaffirs, I was to select a more convenient time for it than when I was for duty. After this I was known by every Kaffir about the Camp. Whenever they saw me they would call out, "Buck, Buck" —a name by which I was known for many years afterwards.

The bush around our Camp was very thick, and all hands were employed daily for some hours in cutting it down and placing it in front of the horses' heads to keep them in line, also to keep the hot winds from them as much as possible as they were very injurious to the horses' eyes.

Some parts of the bush near us were infested with monkeys. The Kaffirs used to bring them to the Camp and sell them for tobacco. Two or three brass buttons or a stick of tobacco would purchase a couple of them. I was informed that the Kaffirs' mode of catching the monkeys was as follows:

A small hole was made in the side of a ripe, sound pumpkin—which grew wild in abundance in the surrounding valley. This would be laid carelessly on the ground where the monkeys were known to frequent. The pumpkin would not remain long before Jacko would find it, and, being exceedingly fond of the seeds, would not hesitate one moment but thrust his hand into the hole to grab a handful of the seed. When he attempts to withdraw it he finds that his hand is much too large for the hole. He has no idea of reducing the size of it by letting go the seed. He will then begin screaming as loud as he is able which brings down all the monkeys in the neighbourhood; and if he was not at once secured by his captors, his friends would soon tear him to pieces in their endeavours to release him. I was never present when they were caught, still I have no reason to doubt this mode as being correct.

The purpose having been accomplished for which the Camp had been formed, we received orders to return to Fort Beaufort. A vast number of Kaffirs came to see us start from the Camp Ground, but their real purpose was to search for brass buttons, of which they are very proud. They wore them as an ornament on a particular part of their body.

Just previous to our leaving the Camp Ground, the attention of most of the Kaffirs appeared to be divided between myself and the man who had been the cause of the woman being burnt to death, since which time not one woman had been seen near our Camp. Nor did the man in question once venture to leave the Camp unless in the company of several others. As each Kaffir recognised the "barber" they shouted as loud as they were able, "Buck, Buck!"

It was nearly dark before we got clear of the Camp Ground and the rain came down very heavy. We had not proceeded far when the discovery was made that we had lost our way. The bush was very thick and soon we found ourselves on the brink of a precipice. We could hear the rush of water beneath us. Everybody, as usual, "knew the way quite well," but at this moment not one knew which direction to take in order to get out of the bush in which we had been floundering about for some time. The Officer Commanding the Infantry said he could get his men through it right enough, so they were allowed to go their own road. We, the Cavalry, were obliged to remain stationary.

The precipice in front, and the bush behind so thick that we could not get the horses through it in the darkness which prevailed, therefore there was no alternative but to remain as we were, holding our horses, until daylight. In this comfortable position we continued for about seven hours before there was sufficient light to enable us to see our way out of the bush.

Shortly after daylight we saw three horsemen riding along a ridge to our right. We hailed them by sounding a trumpet, when they beckoned us to come towards them. I never knew a Colonist that would go one inch out of his way to oblige anyone connected with the Army. Why it was so, I cannot say. However, when we approached we found the horse men to be three Missionaries who were well known to all of us— Mr. Calderwood, Mr. Livingstone and Mr. Moffat. The latter had lived at Fort Beaufort for some years, and Mr. Livingstone was a constant visitor at his house.

Mr. Moffatt said: "Good morning, Captain Croft. Where are you going?"

Captain Croft: "We are going to Fort Beaufort."

Mr. M.: "Not the way you were going surely, as it is quite in the opposite direction. Keep along the ridge and cross the valley to your right. You are about 8 miles from Beaufort."

Captain C.: "Where are you going thus early?"

Mr. M.: "We are going to drop Mr. Calderwood at Block Drift. Me and my son-in-law are going a long journey."

Captain Croft shook hands with each of them and they went on their way. We had crossed the ridge and were crossing the valley to the left, then everyone "knew we had been taking the wrong direction." At length we reached Fort Beaufort.

The Infantry had better have stayed with us as they had wandered about the bush all night and did not reach the Fort for some hours after us; and a considerable portion of their clothing had been torn from their backs in forcing their way through the bush. Previous to leaving the Camp Ground the Commissariat Officer advised the Commanding Officer to take the same road as the waggons which conveyed the stores, camp equipage, etc.

"Oh, no," said the Officer, "we shall take the bush for it and be in Beaufort hours before the waggons get there." But, as it happened, the whole of the waggons were in 9 hours before any of the Troops arrived.

Education in my Regiment was at a very low standard indeed. There were six Troop Sergeant Majors, and it was part of their duty to keep the accounts of the men of their respective Troops. There were three of them could but barely write their name; and (for any person) to at once state what the total amount was for 30 or 31 days at one penny (a day) without the aid of a ready reckoner, would be such an astounding feat in arithmetic as would completely stagger them. Therefore in order to overcome this little educational deficiency, one Private in each Troop was excused a portion of his regular duty—that is to say, his comrades had to do it for him—while he assisted the Troop Sergeant Major in his extensive and intricate calculations, which seldom or never exceeded the knowledge of such as 30 or 31 days at 1d., 2d., or 6d. as the case might be.

I remember shortly after I joined the Regiment a young man, being pointed out to me—he was the son of a Troop Sergeant Major—as being the greatest arithmetician in the Regiment, not even excepting the Regimental Schoolmaster or Mistress. My informant said:

"He can go into fractions like steam—tell you in about five minutes what is the value of $5/8$ of £1. There's no mistake; he's a clever fellow."

My friend "Susan" got the appointment of Assistant Clerk to the Sergeant Major of our Troop. Poor fellow, he was well suited for that but he really was not fit for a soldier. He was almost as helpless on the back of a horse now as he was the first day he mounted.

I remained at Fort Beaufort only a few days, then was sent on detachment to join Colonel Somerset's Division at Camp Barrooka. The bush was thick and swarming with wolves and jackals. Snakes were frequently caught in the Camp. We could not keep our tents clear of scorpions, and at night we were worried nearly to death by mosquitoes and sand fleas. Take it all together, the Camp was most unhealthy. The water for the Troops, which was obtained from a stagnant pool, was of the colour and consistency of cream. There was a spring of beautiful water near the Camp, but the quantity it yielded was so small that it was kept exclusively for the Officers.

There were two Officers in the Cape Mounted Rifles—Captain O'Reilly and Ensign Gordon Cumming. Each of those Officers was always endeavouring to get up some kind of amusement for the Troops in Camp. Either of those Officers could throw the assagai farther and with greater accuracy than any Kaffir I ever saw. Ensign Cumming was very fond of all kinds of athletic games; in fact, his love of them very often got him "dragged over the coals" for being absent from duty or late for parade.

I have seen him repeatedly take off his cap and hang it on a bush, and at a distance of 60 yards would throw the assagai and strike the cap four times out of six. When he wanted a larger target at a greater distance he would take off his jacket, hang it on a bush, and very soon it would be converted into rags.

"Young Hopeful," as he was called, was always in trouble. He never could be on parade in time. Long after the trumpet had sounded Young Hopeful would be seen making his way toward the parade, putting his accoutrements on as he came and invariably two or three Kaffir dogs following him. And his Hottentot servant, who was a Private in the Cape Mounted Rifles, bringing up the rear. Many a time the poor "Totty" was ordered punishment for the faults of his Master, when Young Hopeful would say: "Never mind, Hendricus, come to me by and by and I'll give you a tot of Cape Smoke."

I really believe the Totty was as careless of his duty as his Master. To hear and see Master and servant at times was really laughable in the extreme—the former throwing the assegai and the latter standing near holding his Master's clothes and accoutrements, waiting to assist in putting them on. Their conversation would run thus:

Master: "Hendricus."

Servant: "Yah myneer."

Master: "Go and hang your cap on that bush. Mine is torn all to pieces."

Servant: "Parade trumpet sounded long time ago, myneer."

Master: "Never mind that. Stick up your cap there for only one throw. We shall be on parade presently."

Servant: "Yah myneer, but me get, punished when me late for parade."

Master: "Here, throw the things down there and go to the D----l, you ugly Hottentot."

A few minutes after Young Hopeful would be seen running along, dressing as he came, then the following conversation might have been heard between him and the Adjutant of the Regiment.

Adjutant: "Mr. Cumming, you are always late for parade. Colonel Somerset is very angry at your repeated neglect of duty."

Mr. Cumming: "Is he, though. I'm very sorry for that. Had no idea it was so late."

Adjutant: "Your cap is not fit, Mr. Cumming, for an Officer to come on parade with."

Mr. Cumming: "Yes, I've riddled it pretty well, haven't I? Must try and get another one to-morrow."

The dull routine of military life in the bush in Camp did not suit Cumming. I believe he was under arrest more than once for neglect of duty. At length he left the Service. Some said he made a virtue of a necessity. However that might be, I can honestly say that I never knew a man more deservedly popular among his brother Officers and the Rank and File of the Regiment than Ensign Gordon Cumming of the

Cape Mounted Rifles. Before we left this Camp it was reported that Gordon Cumming had gone on a shooting excursion to the interior.

Here also I had a very narrow escape from getting into serious disgrace. I was on guard, and as things were anything but quiet in the Colony, additional precautions were necessary in Camp, particularly at night.

One morning I was on sentry duty from 3 to 5. It had been a fearful night. The hot winds were enough to choke one, the bush was very thick, and my eyes were very bad. In fact, I was nearly blinded with the hot sand, and several times was obliged to put my hand over my eyes to protect them. In this position, I must have been seen by the Field Officer on duty, who went to the guard tent and ordered the Sergeant to make me a prisoner for sleeping on my post— the punishment for which in time of war used to be death.

When the Sergeant came to me I challenged him at the proper time and in the usual manner—"Who comes there?" He informed me that I was a prisoner by order of the Field Officer, who came shortly after and asked the Sergeant if I had been asleep when he came to me. The Sergeant said I had challenged him at the proper time and was sure I was not asleep, to which the men who were with him would swear.

The Orderly Officer came up and heard the charge against me, also the evidence of the Sergeant. He told the Field Officer I was one of the best soldiers in the Regiment and he felt sure I was not guilty of such gross neglect of duty. At length I was allowed to resume my duty and this acted as a caution to me during the whole of my term of service. Had the Field Officer been of the Cape Mounted Rifles I should not have had the shadow of a chance.

Although the two Regiments went through a great deal together, there never was much love between them. Although the Cape mounted Rifles acted as a Cavalry Regiment, they only ranked as Infantry, and it was said that our arrival in the Colony had brought a considerable amount of extra work on them in the shape of monthly returns, etc., which had been hitherto to them unknown; also it was scarcely known at the War Office that there was such a Corps in existence as the Cape Mounted Rifles.

If all was true, as said the Hottentot Privates of the Regiment, the poor Totties derived considerable benefit from our being near them, in the shape of having their monthly accounts more correctly kept as now they had a little to receive at each monthly settlement; before they had nothing. For instance, if during the month the Totty had drawn a new pair of shoes from the Store, his account would be read to him thus:

"Two pair of felt scoons."—Leather shoes. The Totty would say:"Nay, myneer, only one pair." then would follow:

"Yes, Johnny, two pair—one pair for this foot and one pair for that foot."

The Totty would reply:

"Oh, yah, yah, myneer."

In consequence of a considerable number of men of my Regiment being incapacitated for duty on account of being laid up with dysentery, and the pool of mud having been exhausted—it had given up even the appearance of water for some time past—it was decided to break up the Camp. Accordingly, we returned to Fort Beaufort.

Shortly after the above it was reported that Gordon Cumming had returned to Graham's Town with two waggons laden with ivory, ostrich feathers and valuable skins, which had been sold and had realised a considerable sum of money, which enabled him to start again, this time with five waggons. His old servant, whose discharge from the Cape Mounted Rifles had been obtained, went with him. Three Officers accompanied him, who had obtained three months' leave of absence for that purpose. We heard later on that two of the Officers very soon returned. They did not like his style of living. The steak off the trunk of an elephant was not exactly to their taste.

Chapter Six
The Charge at Zwart Kopjies

March, 1845. War was declared against the Dutch Boers beyond the Orange River. A Division, consisting of Cavalry, Artillery and Infantry, was hastily formed. Waggons, bullocks and drivers were secured and we were ordered to proceed by forced marches to the Dutch Settlements. Infantry had already gone on from other stations farther up country.

Our horses and oxen were in splendid condition and we got on remarkably well. The grass was very good and abundant. The horses required only a small portion of corn, and the oxen lived entirely on grass.

Nothing unusual occurred until after we crossed the Orange River, when all farm houses we came near that were not inhabited were plundered by the Troops, as the owners of them had gone to join the rebels, taking with them all their horses, sheep, cattle, horse waggons and all the best of their furniture; and leaving behind the rest of their farm stock. Being under orders for a forced march—that is, get on as quickly as possible—there was not much time allowed for plundering. Still it was invariably sufficient to enable each of us to get a turkey, goose, fowl or duck; and occasionally we made time to kill a pig or two.

Our mode of procedure was as follows: On sighting a farm house, if within a mile of our track, 20 or 30 men from each Corps of the Division would be allowed to go and seek for plunder, the whole under the command of the Provost Marshal—the terror of evildoers. No ammunition was allowed to be used, and no buildings to be set on fire.

Within two minutes of our reaching the farm it would present a comical sight. Cocks, hens, ducks, turkeys, geese, guinea fowl and pigeons would be flying in all directions, dogs barking and pigs screaming; while those inside the house would be smashing open boxes, drawers or anything else that might contain anything of value.

A few minutes only were allowed for plundering when the order was given to cease and instantly every man took his place, to return in the same orderly manner he had come. Woe betide the man that would venture to stay another instant after the order to cease had been given. After joining their respective Corps the booty was divided, and in a few minutes we were on the move again.

The country we marched through was truly beautiful. It abounded in game deer of various kinds. I really believe I have seen as many as two thousand in one drove. There was no difficulty in shooting them whatever. Venison in those days was at a discount. The fact was the meat was so hard. We had no chance of hanging it for a few days, and we did not stay long enough in one place to boil it sufficiently to soften it.

The men of each tent had provided themselves with a hand mill for grinding wheat. These were got at the different farm houses we plundered together with plenty of wheat. Our beef and mutton were the finest I ever saw out of England. In short, we had a jolly time of it along the road and lived like fighting cocks.

At length we arrived at Philippolis—Griqua town—and a few hours after I took a bit of a ramble to have a look at the place, which I found consisted of one long street. Women and children were lying about on the ground, and their only occupation, as far as I could see, was the searching of each other's heads for vermin. Their habitations were long sheds, and did not appear to contain any kind of partition, bedding or furniture whatever. Their clothing was made of buckskin. The hair of the women long and matted, and by their filthy appearance I should say they never had any connection with soap and water for cleansing purposes.

And these were our allies! The people we had come all this distance to fight for against the Dutch Boers, who had made several raids and plundered them of great numbers of cattle, sheep and goats! Such was their report, but I believe they were too lazy to look after their cattle. The stench of the place was horrible, and I was glad when I got to the end of the "town."

I walked a short distance to get a little fresh air before attempting to go through it again. The country around as far as the eye could reach appeared a vast plain—no grass, but a kind of stubble weed of reddish colour which was very fattening for cattle.

I was returning to the Camp by a different route when suddenly I heard a voice which emanated from an Englishman beyond a doubt:

"Good day to you, sir."

The words startled me. Who would think of meeting an Englishman in this nest of filth? However, such was the case. On looking around from whence the voice proceeded I observed a young man about 28 years of age standing at the door of a shed on which was written *Negotie Winkle*—Retail Store.

After a few words of conversation he invited me into his house—a building 45 feet in length, 14 feet in breadth and 12 feet in height, which contained the shop, one sitting room and two bedrooms. He also had a very large piece of ground under cultivation. His name was Charles Webster. He was a native of Nottingham; had been 12 years in the country, 5 of which in this desolate place. His father and two of his brothers were in the same line of business on the Eastern Frontiers. He traded in coffee, sugar and tobacco by barter in skins, ivory, ostrich feathers and gum, in fact anything that came his way. He had two waggons then on the road to Colesberg—the nearest European settlement—each laden with skins, wool, ostrich feathers and about half a ton of ivory. He expected their contents to realise over £100.

The last Englishman he saw was some months back—a gentleman with two waggons who was going on a shooting excursion. My friend said he had sold the gentleman some very fine skins and feathers This must have been Gordon Cumming going on his first trip.

We had a long and very pleasant conversation. I promised to spend an hour or two with him in the evening and we were to smoke a pipe together, but I was prevented from keeping my promise in consequence of being unexpectedly ordered for duty. On the following evening, however, I came. We had a pipe and a cup of most beautiful coffee. He asked me if I was fond of music; and on telling him I was, he said he was teaching his girls to sing.

"Then you are married?" said I.

"Oh, no," he replied. "They are my servants."

He took down a buckskin bag from the wainscot and took out a very nice looking violin. The moment he touched the instrument I knew he was a musician. He said:

"My stock of music is not very extensive; that book contains all I possess."

It was not a very large one, still it contained some very good music. He played the overture to "William Tell" most beautifully, after which he called in the two servants. Between them and their sisters in the town that I saw engaged in their interesting but filthy occupation, there was a very pleasing contrast, both in their manners and the cleanliness of their persons. When he spoke to them it was in a tone and manner that, were it not for their dusky hue, one could easily fancy he was addressing two of his sisters.

Mr. Webster and the two girls sang "Home, Sweet Home," after which he said "Now we shall have my mother's favourite," and they sang "Cherry Ripe."

It being near 8 p.m. it was time for me to return to the Camp. On leaving, Mr. Webster made me a present of a very handsome *kaross*—a number of skins sewn together. I can safely say that I never spent two happier hours in the whole course of my life. I promised to pay him another visit should the opportunity offer.

On reaching Camp, I learned that an order had been

given for the Cavalry to move at midnight. Why we had remained here thus long was a puzzle to most of us. All hands were quite elated at the possibility of a brush with the Boers who had brought us this long distance. But before midnight the order was countermanded. The Infantry left the camp the next evening, and the following night the whole of the Cavalry and Artillery. After a stiffish march of eighteen hours, some part of which at a gallop, we came up with the Infantry, and the whole Division halted.

The Cavalry were ordered to remove the bridles from their horses but not the saddles, and not to remove our own accoutrements. It was evident that something was on the move, more particularly when the order was given: "Look around your girths and see they are all right."

After a time, the Cavalry and Artillery were ordered to bridle up and move forward. The Infantry had gone on about an hour before. We rode along very steadily and passed the Infantry. Suddenly I heard some order given to the Artillery. I saw the four guns placed rapidly in front. *Bang! Bang! Bang! Bang!* from the Artillery, then came the order: "Dragoons to the front. Front, form line. Draw swords!" The trumpet sounded the "Charge" and away we went.

I cannot say that I remember how I felt. We were enveloped in a cloud of dust and I heard a couple of shells go whistling over our heads, besides numerous bullets. Anything beyond that, I did not have any thought of.

But I was suddenly brought to recollection by my head and shoulders coming in sharp contact with the ground. My beautiful charger had got both his fore legs into one of those dangerous holes made by the ant bear. For a moment I was very much afraid that Spider had broken his neck. It was some time before I could persuade him to move and I really thought it was all over with him. But he very unexpectedly gave me to understand that such was not the case by springing to his feet and dashing both his hind legs at me in a most spiteful manner. But I expect he must have forgotten the length of time I had been under his tuition. I was prepared for him. I jumped on his back and galloped to the front.

By the time I arrived there the action of *Zwart Kopjies*— Black Rocks—was over and the Boers were beaten. 230 surrendered as prisoners,and a great number escaped in their 6 and 8 horse waggons across the plain. We could have pursued and cut off their retreat, but there was a motive for letting them escape this time;besides, we had quite sufficient to occupy us for the present in securing what we had already captured, which was considerable, consisting of 230 prisoners, 18,000 sheep and goats, 4,000 head of fine cattle, 30 waggons each with 6 horses, 48 sacks of gunpowder, 420 stand of arms, 2 12 lb. howitzers, and a number of shells.

Among the prisoners we found two deserters from the 91st—Argylshire—Regiment. Their names were James Lapping and Robert Hill.They had been appointed by the Rebels as Captains of Artillery. When taken prisoners they had just bolted from the guns, from which they had been discharging shell at the very Regiment from which they had deserted about two years previous. When they were recognized by the men of the 91st, the Officers had the greatest difficulty in restraining the men of the Regiment from taking the law into their own hands and shooting them on the spot.They were placed under a strong guard, and an Officer was always present to protect them from the men of their own Regiment.

Information was received the same evening of the Rebels having another Camp in which they were well entrenched, about 7 miles hence. It was also stated that the Boers' Camp was nearly surrounded by pitfalls. It was the opinion of the spy that the attempt should not be made that night. The Troops had had quite enough for one day—the Infantry in particular.They had been 20 hours on the march without a mouthful of food, therefore our further movements were postponed until the following morning.

Some of us fared pretty well with what we found in the captured waggons. Me and my comrade managed to find in one waggon a pot full of meat, several loaves of beautiful bread, and plenty of coffee and sugar. By the manner in which the interior of the waggon was laid out, we were under the impression that a party of six or seven were on the point of sitting down to their evening meal when we came in sight and thus disturbed them. Well, they ought to have been thankful that it was not wasted. I am sure me and my comrade done our best to give due honour to the spread.

The following morning at daybreak we were on the move again to attack the Rebel Camp; but had not proceeded above one mile when we saw several men riding towards us, two of them bearing a white flag each. They came to inform us that they would surrender and they had a narrow escape from meeting with a very warm reception by being blown to atoms. The Artillery ran their guns out and prepared for action and was on the point of firing on the flag of truce when the discovery was made that no order had been given to that effect. The fact was this. The Officer in command of the Artillery, Captain Shepherd, was quite deaf, in fact so much so that anyone would need to speak very loud in order to make him hear. Yet most singular to relate, there was one man in the Battery, a Farrier—his name was Darling—Captain Shepherd could always hear this man when speaking in a very moderate tone of voice, but if the man was not with him, he appeared lost, and thus it was on this occasion. I expect he saw the Dutchmen coming over the plain and thought he had a right to have a shot at them. The Boers appeared somewhat scared for a moment, then continued to advance. They said they would surrender.

The Cavalry went off at a gallop to take possession of the Camp, arms and ammunition. It was fortunate we did not attempt to take it the night before or it might have been a tough job. Their Camp was a square formed of waggons two deep and surrounded by a trench 8 feet deep, and numerous pitfalls. We took possession of their arms, ammunition, and about 20 sacks of gunpowder, 46 waggons and about 250 horses. A sufficient number of waggons only were taken from them to convey the arms, &c., to *Zwart Kopjies*, the remainder were left in their possession pending instructions from Cape Town, and we returned to our Camp of the previous night.

The following day the two deserters were tried by General Court Martial; and on the following day, Sunday, their sentence was promulgated in the presence of the whole of the Troops in Camp. Robert Hill was sentenced to be shot, and James Lapping to transportation for life.

After the Court Martial had been read a sermon was preached by the Chaplain, the Reverend. Brownlow Maitland, Private Chaplain to the General, Sir Peregrine Maitland. The subject of the text was "Judas, the Betrayer." Of the Troops present all were more or less affected by the impressive discourse of the Chaplain, but the conduct of the prisoners was disgraceful, more particular that of Hill, who continued laughing the whole time the Sermon was being preached.

The firing party had been told off. The carbines loaded with ball cartridge except one that was loaded with blank. That is done in order that no man can say positively "I shot him in such a place." The carbines are taken from the firing party and loaded by one man, and he himself does not know into whose carbine he has put the blank.

All were under the impression that the sentence would be carried out immediately after the sermon, as every preparation for it had been made, even to the digging of the grave.

Yet it was plain to be seen the struggle that was going on in the breast of the General between justice and mercy. At length the latter gained the ascendancy, and the General addressed the prisoners in the most feeling manner in reference to the enormity of the crime of which they had been guilty.

Desertion was bad enough, but worse when men not only deserted but took up arms against their Sovereign. But their crime was still worse as they, had, in addition to all this, taken up arms and fired on their comrades of the very Regiment from which they had deserted. However much he might be acting against the wishes of a great many present and also his duty to his Country, he was vested with the power to commute the death sentence and he would carry it out with mercy. His heart would not allow him to hurry a man into eternity so entirely unprepared as the prisoner.

Here Hill said something to Lapping and they both laughed. The General took no notice of it but continued to address them. He would take the responsibility on himself to spare the convict's life, pending Her Majesty's pleasure.

Had the men of their own Regiment been selected for the firing party, I believe they would have been shot in spite of the General.

I may here remark that just as my horse fell in the charge, a shell burst very near me that had been fired by one of those fellows. It would not have surprised me at any moment to have heard that they had been shot, as the feeling of the men of their Regiment was so much against them; not in particular for desertion, but in pointing their guns exactly over the position occupied by their former comrades.

Chapter Seven
My Time Among the Boers

After things had become somewhat settled we had the opportunity of resting a while. The General very often dined with the Officers, and on these occasions a number of men, of which I was invariably the head, were selected for the purpose of singing for their amusement. My songs were extempore or of my own composition on passing events. I shall not attempt to say that either would bear much criticism, still they answered the purpose intended, namely, to pass a pleasant hour.

At length, the terms of peace having been settled— much more favourably for the Boers than they expected—nearly all their horses, waggons, arms, ammunition and cattle were returned to them. The two howitzers were not.

The beginning of July we started from Dutchland for Fort Beaufort by a route different to the one we came by. The farm houses were all occupied, and I had several opportunities of proving the boundless hospitality of the Dutch Boers. One of our guides once said when we were on the road up, in reference to plundering the Dutch homesteads: "You don't know the Dutch Boers or you would not inflict unnecessary punishment on their families." Truly he spoke; we did not know them. We seldom passed more than one farm each day, when two or three men would be allowed to go and see if they had anything for sale such as eggs, butter or cheese. They always gave whatever they could spare and would not take anything for it. The farms were far distant from each other in consequence of the scarcity of water. The cleanliness of the interior of their houses could not be surpassed.

After crossing the Orange River the first settlement we

reached was Colesberg, inhabited principally by Dutch. We remained there two days. The last night, one of our men who had been introduced into the house of the *Drostdy*— magistrate—by a Hottentot servant, broke into the wine cellar and, when the owner put in appearance the man struck him several times and knocked him down. The Dutchman called for help and the man was secured and handed over to the civil power. The following day he was tried and sentenced to six months' imprisonment with hard labour in the gaol of Colesberg.

This man was one of the smartest soldiers in the Regiment, but for some time past had given way to drink. In fact, he never let the opportunity pass of getting drunk. He was reported to be the natural son of a Colonel in the Army. A great deal of money was sent him from time to time, but he spent it all in drink. This man finished a long career of crime when he was hanged at Newgate Prison December 15th, 1856. His name was Robert Marley.

Shortly after leaving Colesberg a valuable horse belonging to one of the Officers met with an accident by getting a sharp pointed bone in his foot. Fortunately we were near to a farm house at the time it happened. After the bone was extracted the horse was quite lame, on the following morning was entirely unable to travel and consequently had to be left behind at the farm house. I was ordered to remain and proceed with it as soon as he was sufficiently recovered to enable him to do so. Instructions were given me by the Veterinary Surgeon what to do with him, and shortly afterwards the Regiment left the Camping Ground.

I then began to think of my position—left with people who did not understand a word I said, and I was nearly as bad with regard to their language. I found the shed was very clean and comfortable and I made up my mind to make it my bedchamber.

Shortly after I was visited by the farmer and one of his daughters—a fine, strapping girl of 17—and after a great deal of sputtering on both sides I recognized the words, "*Scoff, myneer*,"—Food, sir.

I was taken into the house and was shown everything that was eatable and drinkable. A portion of each was offered me. I accepted a loaf of bread and some *Bel tongue*—preserved beef. A large earthern vessel containing coffee was placed in front of me, and I made a hearty meal.

The family consisted of the farmer, his wife—the fattest woman I ever saw, who appeared to take a great liking to me as, after shaking hands, she offered her cheek for me to kiss. There was three sons and four daughters. It was the youngest that came with her father to the stable. Of the whole family there was only one who could speak English, and he was away shooting.

In the evening I retired to my chamber—shed—and prepared for sleep. It did not take long to make my bed as I was not troubled with a superfluity of bed clothing. When I had settled down for the night, one of the sons brought me another bowl of coffee.

I was up early the following morning, but I found those in the house had risen before me and all busy at work. I spent a couple of hours fomenting and dressing the horse's foot, after which I took a walk around the farm.

The house consisted of a long shed divided into different apartments, beginning with the kitchen or living room and ending with the best bedroom. There is one room "The Best Room"—this is only used on special occasions as weddings, christenings, and when the house is visited by the Dutch Minister, which is not very often.

I made a very hearty breakfast of bread, butter, eggs and coffee. In the afternoon I was visited by the Field Cornet—District Magistrate—who asked me several questions in reference to the horse and other matters, and said he would come and see me again in a couple of days.

Shortly after he left, the fat lady was showing me some things in the best room when the youngest daughter ran to the door and began calling out very loud, which was immediately taken up by all in the house. The old man took me to the door and pointed with his finger across the plain. It was the son returning home. They were all very pleased of his coming because he could speak English.

He was embraced by his mother and sisters as soon as he dismounted, after which I was introduced to him. He was about 27 years of age, 6 ft.in height, and very strong looking. We shook hands and he bade me welcome to — Kop.

If they were kind to me before he arrived, now they were doubly so. Petre was proud indeed of the opportunity he had now of showing his sisters how well he could speak English. I could not say much for the quality of it myself as occasionally I was put to my wit's end to know what he was talking about, but after a little time I could understand him very well. He informed me that their Minister was coming the next day. I fancied there was some extra amount of cleaning going on in the house. I spent another couple of hours fomenting my lame charge, and was glad to find that he was able to stand on the bad foot.

At sunset all the cattle was brought in and enclosed in *Kraals*—large circles formed of the mimosa tree. Beyond the Orange River, where bush was scarce, stone walls are built for the purpose. Petre informed me that his father was the owner of 10,000 sheep bred for the wool. I had often laughed when I heard of sheep having trucks behind them to support the tail; some hundreds might be seen here with tail trucks.

Our evening meal consisted of *Bel tongue*, bread, fresh butter, eggs and coffee, finishing the evening with a pipe and a cup of peach brandy punch. About 9 o'clock I retired to my couch, coiled myself up in my cloak and horse blanket, and went to sleep.

I arose the following morning at sunrise. The day was Sunday. The Minister had arrived during the past night and several families were expected to join in the Service. I was told that sometimes they will travel a considerable distance in order to meet their Minister.

My first job was to look after my horse. I walked him about for some little time, then I put the saddle on him and gave him a canter across the plain; after which I concluded that he would be fit to travel the next day should the Field Cornet visit me as promised.

On my return to the stable I was visited by my friend Petre and his sister, who came to ask me if I would like to attend prayers with them. I replied that I should very much indeed, and requested that I be allowed to take my breakfast in the stable as there were so many visitors in the house.

Breakfast being over, I began to consider what I had to do. There was one thing certain, that if I wished to appear any way tidy before the company, it would be necessary for me to turn laundress for a time. I must candidly admit my wardrobe was rather meagre, and as I had but little time to spare I made my way at once to a small stream of water and began operations. But I had not been there many minutes when I heard a voice and, looking round, I found a Hottentot girl standing near.

She gave me to understand that she would assist me if I would allow her. I recognized her as one of the servants at the house, and about the most ordinary looking Totty I ever saw and of the purest Hottentot breed.

All attended prayers at the time appointed. I was placed by the side of the fat old lady, and the youngest daughter on the other side of me. Petre said I ought to "feel great honour," and so I did.

I should think there were about 30 present, of both sexes. The Service was in the Dutch language. I could not understand one word of it. However, I stood up when the rest did and the same in kneeling, and I am perfectly satisfied that I felt more devout than I have many a time when I have been obliged to stand and listen to a Sermon of one hour's duration, nearly choked with a leather collar buttoned up tight as though in a vice, and loaded like a donkey.

At the conclusion of the Service there was some singing such as I had never heard before. It was simple but very pretty. Petre played the flute very nicely. After the Service concluded, all partook of refreshment, and some of the old Dutchmen had a pipe and some brandy punch, and within one hour most of them had taken their departure.

Me, Petre, Andries and Hendricus went for a ride, as I wished to try my horse again to see if he was really fit to travel as I was anxious to be moving. While riding I remarked to my friend Petre the great distance there was between each farm on these extensive plains. He said it was in consequence of the scarcity of water. Nearly all the springs in that part of the country were brakish and entirely unfit for use, but wherever there was fresh water to be got there would surely be a house, and at this time there was little or nothing to pay for the land. When a Boer built a house he considered the land as far as he could see all round was his property, and should another build a house within sight of him he would be looked upon as encroaching on the property of another.

We returned in time for dinner. Grace was said by the Minister, which was interpreted to me by Petre—whether correctly or not I cannot say. The substance of which was that while we study the welfare of the soul we should not forget the welfare of the body. And there is no mistake but his portly appearance was quite sufficient to convince anyone he was not guilty of forgetting the latter, however much he might be of the former.

After dinner I took a walk with the three sons and two of the daughters. Petre said they were all much surprised at the progress I had made in my knowledge of their language. Although I had been among them three days, I began to understand them very well. Had I been as old then as I am now, the progress I then made would not have surprised me. As many of you, I make no doubt are aware, the progress of a pupil often depends on the kind of tutor they may have.

Several times during the walk Petre was asked by his youngest sister to interpret to her what I had been talking about. In short they all wanted that, and so rapid did one question succeed another that one half of them were unanswered; and I dare say, in the hurry to interpret, the wrong answer was applied to the question put.

They were most anxious in their enquiries about the Royal Family. Had I ever seen the Queen? And did she live happily with her husband? Some of the questions put to me were comical in the extreme.

After returning from our walk I again examined my horse, and was pleased yet sorry to find that he was quite able to travel. Yes, I was sorry at the idea of leaving a place where I had experienced more happiness during the last three days than in the whole three years which preceded it.

After the evening meal I found that the Minister could speak English very well, and we had a pleasant conversation, in which my friend Petre was not a little proud to be able to join. I am sure his sister was quite as proud to hear him. Before retiring to rest I wished Petre to inform his father that it was my intention to leave them on the following day, should the Field Cornet make his visit early in the day.

When my host was informed of my intended departure on the morrow he said several times, "*Nay, myneer.*"- No, sir. He wished me to remain a few days longer. He would take me for a day's shooting. They were all willing to do anything if I would stay a few days longer with them; even the fat old lady whose voice I had heard but once—that was when she bade me welcome on my first appearance in the house—endeavoured to persuade me to stay.

Petre said he had been looking at the horse and was of opinion that it would be safer if I gave him two or three days more rest. Sanna asked her brother to do his best to persuade me to stay as we had been so happy together. The Minister also joined them in endeavouring to persuade me to prolong my stay.

I said I thanked them all very much for their kindness, and explained to them through the Minister that every day I remained left me one day further from the Regiment in a strange country where I could not understand a dozen words of the language. My host said that should be no obstacle; that no matter how far the Regiment might be, I should have a safe escort. I begged to decline his very kind offer.

My decision appeared to cast a damper on all of them. they were under the impression that I was not satisfied with my food, or they were not sufficiently kind to me. Was there anything they could do for me? Again I declined, after which there was very little said during the remainder of the evening. About 10 p.m. I retired to the stable. It was my own express wish to sleep in the stable in order to be near the horse I had in charge.

I rose early the next morning and shortly afterward was visited by the Field Cornet, who examined the horse and was of the same opinion as myself, namely, that he was quite well enough to travel and would send me a guide to take me to the Regiment. But my host said he would make the necessary arrangement, which was accepted. Some few words passed between them before the Field Cornet left. Petre told me that the latter had asked his father how I had behaved during my stay.

It was arranged that Andreas should start at once, leading my horse and riding one of his own to a farm about 20 miles hence, and my host would lend me a horse to go that distance or farther if I wished. This would enable me to stay a few hours longer before I started. As I thought the suggestion most excellent, I gladly accepted the offer. It would be lighter for my horse, also enable him to have a few hours rest before I reached him.

At length the time came for parting, and a sad one it was. Had I been their own son they could not have treated me with greater kindness. I saw tears run from the eyes of the fat old lady when she offered her cheek for me to kiss. I thought more of that than all their previous kindness.

But where was Sanna? I looked around; all were there but not her. Petre said she was in great grief and could not bid me goodbye. I never saw her again. The last farewell was spoken— and I am sure I shall never forget the kindness I experienced beneath the roof of Petre Andries Venvogle of — Kop.

Before we had proceeded 100 yards, Petre was called back by his father, with whom he remained in conversation for some few minutes. When he joined me we made a fair start, and, both being well mounted, went over the ground at a pretty good pace.

When we reached the next farm I found that Andreas had been in about 4 hours. The horse was quite fresh and not at all lame. Both my friends were well known at the farm, and we were supplied with all we required. The next farm was only 15 miles distant, and as Andreas was willing to go on with my horse I decided to rest a couple of hours, then push on in order to reach there about sunset. I was most agreeably surprised when I was informed that it was their uncle who occupied the next farm, which we reached shortly after sunset.

As my shoulder was aching very much, I examined my haversack to see what it contained as it felt somewhat heavy. I found it had been filled with *Bel tongue*, bread and a small jar of fresh butter; and, wrapped in a piece of cloth, was a small white handkerchief, in the corner of which were the initials S. V.

I was informed by Petre's uncle that the Regiment could not be more than one good day's ride from here, and there was a good road for guidance the whole distance. I was glad to hear this. The following morning I bade my friends Petre and Andreas good-bye.

The former said he had been desired by his father to ask me if I should like to leave the Army and live with them. His father would purchase my discharge if I could send him word that such was my wish. I gave him my word that I would write to his father, and we parted; but not before Andreas had taken a knife from his pocket which he pressed me to accept it in remembrance of him.

Chapter Eight
Return to the Regiment

I came up to the Regiment at sunset. The horse was all right and not at all lame. The Officer was much pleased and said he had not expected to see the horse under a month, and gave me a sovereign.

The Regiment had made an attempt that morning to cross the neck of the Winterberg Mountain, but had been driven back by the snow and had to repitch their tents where the snow was two feet deep, and no wood to be had for cooking or warmth. Thanks to my late friends, I had in my haversack a good stock of bread, meat and butter, a portion of which I gave to my comrades.

We remained in this cold, desolate place two days when another attempt was made somewhat more successful, but the wind was very high, and the sleet blew down from the mountain which stung us about our hands and face fearfully. The snow was deep on the ground. Those who chose to ride, did so. Several men were nearly barefooted, their boots had been rotted off their feet in the snow and the "Gentlemen" Dragoons presented a most pitiable sight.

At length we reached the district of Somerset, having been 22 hours getting over the Winterberg. The distance we had travelled was 54 miles. The first 17 hours were through snow; the last 5 hours we were crossing the lower range into the valley, where we halted.

There was a small Fort held by a detachment of the 27th Regiment. Some sheep were procured for us and were very soon slaughtered. In less than one hour from the time of arrival the horses were all fed, fires were burning in all directions, tin pots of water were boiling and lumps of mutton frizzling on the numerous fires that were scattered about. The Regiment having been nearly three days without food, the consumption was enormous.

Having satisfied our appetites, we lay on the ground, our saddle for a pillow, the canopy of heaven our covering, and soon all were fast asleep. I have no doubt the fatigue of the last few days added materially to the depth of our slumbers; but what a wonderful contrast between this and only 24 hours previous, when we were nearly frozen and here we were lying about on the ground like a flock of sheep. A more rapid transit from winter to summer I should think could not possibly be made.

We remained here the following day, although within ten miles of our destination. This was in order to procure some articles of clothing, as some of the men were literally in rags and some entirely without boots and it would not look altogether the thing to see a lot of Dragoons march into the Fort in that state, so we had to wait until the necessary articles were sent for.

The following day we marched into Fort Beaufort, and the three following days were given us by the Commanding Officer to enjoy ourselves after the campaign.

October, 1845. For some time past one of the Officers of my Regiment, Captain Bambrick, had been very kind to me. He had introduced me to Mrs. Ward, wife of Captain Ward of the 91st Regiment. This lady was a great contributor to the Cape papers, also to several magazines at home. On one occasion I was taken by Captain Bambrick to sing at a party given by this lady in honour of her daughter's birthday. I have every reason to be proud of the great kindness I received from that lady.

At another time a party was given by Captain Ward at which I was also present, and had obtained leave to remain from Barracks until 11 p.m. Captain Bambrick was one of the party. About 11 o'clock I took leave of the company and hastened to the Guardhouse to report my arrival to the Sergeant of the Guard. He informed me that the Regimental

Sergeant Major had given an order to the effect that my leave was only to 11 o'clock, and if I was not there by 11.15 he was to make me a prisoner when I did return for overstaying my leave.

As it was 11.25 when I reached the Guardhouse, the Sergeant had no alternative but to keep me there a prisoner. During the night I was told by one of the Guard that, when the R.S.M. was informed I had gone to sing at a party, he said he would see if he could not put a stop to my spouting for Officers. I never knew a man more embittered against his superiors than he was, yet he was daily expecting a Commission himself when he also would become an Officer.

The following morning I sent to Captain Bambrick to inform him of my arrest, also to beg his attendance at the Office when I should be brought before the Commanding Officer, in order that he might state my whereabouts during my absence.

Shortly afterwards Captain Bambrick came to the Guardhouse to see me. He said very little, but I could see he was very much annoyed. He told me he would see the Commanding Officer and explain the cause of my absence. At 11 a.m. I was taken to the C.O. and was at once released without one word of censure or explanation. But I know the R.S.M. got a word or two for keeping me a prisoner 12 hours for overstaying my leave 25 minutes.

In consequence of several complaints having been made by duty men of the number of men in some Troops that were exempt from certain duties in order to assist the Troop Sergeant Majors in performing their manifold duties, an order was issued that in future no man was to be exempt from duty for such purpose. The consequence was that "Susan" lost his appointment as assistant clerk to the T.S.M. Although he received nothing for it, it got him out of many an ugly job. I saw him one morning when I was going down to the stables. He was sitting on a bag containing corn near the Commissariat Store, whither he had been sent to draw corn for the Troop horses.

I said:"Hello, 'Susan,' what are you sitting there for?"

He replied:"I am waiting for someone to help me carry this corn."

I asked:"How much does it weigh?"

He answered:"106 lbs. and the bag."

The latter weighed about two pounds. At length he said:

"If someone don't come and help me, I shall leave it and go to the Doctor and get excused from carrying such a weight." Addressing me: "Buck, I'll give you a stick of tobacco if you'll carry it for me."

I carried it for him, but he was well able to carry it himself. He was three inches taller than I and weighed nearly two stone more, but he was very lazy.

December, 1845. I joined an Amateur Theatrical Club. An old building having been given over to us by the Barrack Master, we soon converted it into a Theatre. We advertised to give three performances. The pieces selected were *The Floating Beacon*, and *The Padlock*. I was to play the part of Mungo, the black servant, in the latter piece.

Our receipts for the first two performances amounted to £37, our expenses £21. The treasurer, a Sergeant of the 91st Regiment, said he had lost £7. On being asked how he had lost it, all the satisfaction we could get was that he had lost it "somehow or somewhere"—which left only £9 to be divided among the members. Then it was proposed that this sum should remain until the third performance was over, when the total sum could be divided. This was agreed upon, but before we could get up the third performance the Barrack Master required the building and we were obliged to clear out.

The timber we had used cost £17. This was sold for £3. The man who bought it bolted from his creditors, so we lost that; and the £9 which should have been divided was not forthcoming. It was quite evident to me that the £9 had gone to seek for the £7 which had disappeared "somehow or somewhere," as our treasurer was not sober for three months.

December 31st, 1845. This evening I was directed to go to Captain Bambrick's house. He wished to see me as I was going away the following morning on detachment to Graham's Town. He wished to give me a little advice—hoped I would take care of myself and endeavour to maintain the same character I had borne hitherto. He would be a friend to me as long as I lived.

It was not likely that he would remain long in the Regiment. He was getting old and would return to England in another year or so, and would take me with him.

He showed me a watch and said:

"You will be at Graham's Town about 12 months. If I hear a good account of you, when you return I will make you a present of this watch; and in the event of my death I have made an entry in my diary that you are to get it from my executors. I do hope you will be a good lad."

These last words he repeated several times. At parting the Captain shook hands with me and gave me three sovereigns, little dreaming what the next six months would bring forward for both of us—his bones bleaching on the plain and me severely wounded.

January 1st, 1846. Was sent on detachment with my Troop to Graham's Town. Shortly after we left the Fort we met Mr. Moffatt, the Missionary, with his constant attendant, Jantze Pete. A more treacherous looking Kaffir I never put eyes on, but the Missionary did not appear to think so. Meeting him caused a delay of about half an hour. Captain Croft and Mr. Moffatt were very intimate. He was a rare one for knocking about Kaffirland, but was seldom away from his home for more than a few days at a time. He was about the best-tempered old man I ever met.

We halted for the night at Koonap, near the River of that name. Here there was a farm house or African hotel. Such places were very necessary, as often when travellers arrived on the banks of these African rivers they would find them so swollen that they could not get across for some days.

We had a very wet march and there was considerable delay in getting corn for the horses. My pretty horse, Spider, must have been in a bad temper, I expect,or hungry perhaps, as he seized me by the left shoulder and gave me a most terrible bite, almost equal to the bite of a camel. So severe was it that I shall carry the marks of it to my grave.

On reaching Graham's Town the following day, I was admitted into Hospital in the greatest agony, but with attention and a few days' rest I soon began to improve, and then redeemed my promise to write to my Dutch friends. The following is a copy of the letter I sent:

Graham's Town,
January 6th, 1846.

My very Dear Friends:

After a long silence, I have at last mustered sufficient courage to redeem my promise of writing to you. You may perhaps have thought I had forgotten you by my long silence, but silence does not at all times necessitate forgetfulness. Forget you, I don't believe I ever shall. The kindness I received at your hands is indelibly fixed on my mind. As I have many times said, had I been a son or brother greater kindness never could have been shown me, not by one alone but by all. Many times I have been on the point of writing when I had thought I had made up my mind what to do; then I would think again and invariably come to a different conclusion.

Dear Mr. Venvogle, I have weighed well over in my mind your more than generous offer, made to me through your son Petre before we parted. I feel sure you would all endeavour to make me feel happy among you, but I have many friends and relations in England whom I wish to see again in a few years hence, but if I should settle at — Kop I must give up all thoughts of such ever taking place.

I have returned the small parcel I found in my haversack. I dare not keep it. It would remind me too often of one whom I must endeavour to forget, but whose future happiness I devoutly pray for. Do not think me ungrateful. I wish I could find words to express what I feel. That is impossible. I shall ever retain a pleasing recollection of the few happy days I spent among you. I trust you ,will ever think of me as the soldier you so much befriended. May God bless you all, and may each of you prosper as you deserve, will ever be the sincere prayer of

Yours
In all sincerity,

W. J. Adams.

I remained in the hospital ten days before I was able to use my arm.

Jan. 24th. Gordon Cumming returned from his second expedition with four waggons laden with ivory, feathers and skins, which were sold in the market place and, according to the *Graham's Town Journal*, realised a good sum of money.

During his stay in Graham's Town he was the guest of Captain Hogg, 7th Dragoon Guards. There is no mistake but he was the "Lion" of the day. Everyone courted his society. I often heard the remark passed that he was more like a "lady killer" than "A Lion Slayer." He had quite a feminine cast of features. During his stay a grand ball was given in honour of his visit. He went in full Highland costume. I had the job of polishing up his silver mounted pistols, sword, dirk and sundry other articles.

February 1st, 1846. Four Kaffir Chiefs came into the town to pay their respects to Gordon Cumming. their names were Maccomo, Pato, Botman and Stock. Many were of opinion that they had some other motive in view and had come to look about them and find out the most vulnerable part of the town where they might attack with the greatest safety when the next Kaffir war should break out. I will endeavour to give a description of these four gentlemen.

Maccomo—about 45 years of age, clad in a very large and handsome *kaross*, a coil of very common large beads around his neck, and on his feet a pair of patent leather Wellington boots with large red tassels hanging down in front of them.

Botman—about 50 years of age. A very dirty looking Kaffir and very stout. He wore an Officer's forage cap, very old; a kind of stage Naval Officer's coat with one very large epaulette on the right shoulder and very long narrow tails to the coat; a pair of trunks reaching to the knees; feet bare.

Stock—about 45 years of age and rather a fine looking man. He wore a gold-laced cap with large gold peak; blue cloth dress coat with epaulettes and any amount of gold lace; patent leather boots with large gold tassels in front; gold lace Cavalry overalls cut off at the knees—I suppose, to show off his boots.

Pato—about 40 years of age, a most repulsive looking fellow. He wore a very old-fashioned Infantry Officer's dress coat minus the tails; blue overalls with gold stripes and low shoes; overalls cut off at the knees.

They were all very much disappointed in their visit to Mr. Cumming. They begged hard for a bottle of brandy, but they did not get it.

The Chiefs took their departure before sunset. People were wondering what they came in for and who had given them liberty, but they must have had permission from the authorities or they would not have attempted to come in "in state."

Chapter Nine
The Kaffirs Prepare for War

Feb. 3rd, '46. I was one of a party of 10 Dragoons and 14 Cape Mounted Rifles who were sent, under the command of Captain Canning of the C.M.R., in search of deserters who were known to be employed in great numbers cutting timber in the immense forest "The Holiphants Hook."

All the timber required for building purposes on the Eastern Frontiers came from this forest. The employers were English and Dutch settlers, mostly the former. These men well knowing those they employ are deserters from the Army, have them at their own price, which is a very low one. The men got plenty to eat and drink—a great deal too much of the latter—and a horse to ride, but not a coin in money. And all this was well known to every soldier in the Colony, yet up to this time no steps whatever had been taken to stop the number of desertions or apprehend the men who were employing them. Their mode of procedure was as follows:

Visit the brandy sheds or grog shops where the soldiers were drinking and call for a lot of brandy or wine; hand it round to the soldiers, tell them to drink, boast of their wealth and throw out a gentle hint that they too were once in the Service but saw a chance of bettering themselves and did so, and there was still the same chance as he had for any man who had pluck in him. The result was invariably that on the following morning there was one or two men absent. The decoy would stay a day or two, get as many as he could, and then disappear and would not be seen at that station again.

The information in this case had been given by an English settler who also acted as our guide. He gave every information in reference to their employment, the huts they lived in and the depravity of the whole of them.How was it this man knew so much about them and why did he give the information? The cause was this.Until recently he had had a large number of men—believed to be deserters—in his employ but they had left him to go and work for another man who offered them wages in addition to board and lodging; and in order to be revenged on the whole of them he had divulged the secret of their retreat.

The route selected by the guide was one by which we were not likely to meet any person, black or white, that could give information of our approach. Such a dangerous path I never travelled before or since. We were all dismounted; the horses had to climb over the rocks like cats. At dusk we halted for rest and refreshment.

We had brought with us three days'food ready cooked,in order that no fires should be made that might attract attention to our movements. Shortly after midnight, the moon being up, we started on again, and at daylight had reached the outskirts of the Forest, where we remained concealed until the evening.

Our guide informed us that the deserters lived in log huts in the most dense parts of the Forest, and which could only be reached by one person at a time through a low and very narrow opening very much like a wolf track. During the time they were in the hut the entrance to the path is guarded by a Hottentot woman with whom the deserters cohabited. The moment a stranger appears, the signal is given which is immediately forwarded by others, and the men in the hut would make their escape from the back into the Forest before anyone could get near enough to identify them.

We could not arrest a man until we had good cause to suspect him as being a deserter, consequently it was necessary to identify a man to a certain extent before we could arrest him. But in reference to those we were after there was no cause for doubt as none but deserters would live in such places.

Feb. 5th. Started again as soon as the moon was up, and before daylight the actions of our guide were somewhat suspicious. He had been missed about three hours the previous day, for which he accounted by saying he went only a short distance from us and then lay down and fell asleep. The Commanding Officer now insisted on going through a part of the bush much against the wish of the guide, who was noticed to be making a peculiar noise between a cough and a growl. It became necessary at last to caution him not to make so much noise.

However daylight came and not a sign of a human being could be seen. There were a great number of trees that had been recently cut down. The guide wished to go a little farther, but the Officer decided to remain where we were and a close watch was kept on the guide, who, it was quite evident, began to regret the part he was taking in the business.

Toward evening one of the Hottentot Riflemen reported that he could hear men singing but as no one else could hear it no notice was taken of it, and we settled down for an hour or two's rest after "supper"—a smoke of the pipe. Many times the same supper fell to my lot.

Feb. 6th. Moved on again about 2 a.m. and the actions of our guide being still somewhat suspicious in spite of repeated cautions, he was made a prisoner and informed by the Commanding Officer that he had power to shoot him if he did not alter his conduct. This caution had the desired effect, and he promised to lead us to the place where the singing had been heard by the Hottentot. He knew well where it came from at the time. He said the place was about 200 yards distant, but it would be impossible to reach the huts until it was daylight. Accordingly, we remained quiet until daybreak.

During the time we were waiting several times we heard the voices of men singing. At length, the party being made up that was to make the attack—consisting of 4 of the 7th Dragoons Guards. and six of the Cape Mounted Rifles—leaving our horses behind we started on foot.

We had not proceeded far when I saw a Hottentot woman fast asleep at the entrance to one of the paths before described. Captain Canning crept softly up to her and clapped a handkerchief over her mouth. When she opened her eyes she found a pistol pointed to her face. The shock was so great that she went into a fit.

We slowly advanced in single file up the path a distance of about 200 yards, when we came in sight of the huts. At this moment a large dog began barking which was immediately shot by the Officer, but not before the noise had aroused those who were inside.

Several made their escape from the back of the huts—of which there were five, each containing two apartments and two beds, about eight Hottentot women and several children. The latter were the most repulsive looking creatures I ever saw. I have been informed that the children of the mixed race of pure Hottentot and English are so.

Two of the men who were not quite so active as their companions were seized at the door of one of the huts. One of them, a very powerful fellow, made a desperate resistance for the moment. He seized hold of one of our men by the legs and threw him clean over his head. He was then brought to subjection by a carbine being pointed to his head and I gave him to understand that it was loaded and should not hesitate, if he were not instantly quiet, to trouble him with a pill that would be more effectual than even one of Morrison's itself. The fellow's name was Smith, but he was better known as Long Tom Coffin. The other man surrendered at once as he was afraid we should not hesitate in shooting them if they were troublesome.

On searching the huts more closely, we found a man concealed beneath some grass in a state of drunkenness, but when he opened his eyes the shock was sufficient to sober him. The three men were conducted beyond the path, and as each of them possessed a horse they were placed on the saddle with their hands tied behind them. This was necessary as Smith had twice before been arrested and each time had escaped from his escort. Three Dragoons and six of the Cape Mounted Rifles were sent as escort with the prisoners to the Prison at Sidbury.

This was exceedingly rough work. The food we had brought with us, which should have lasted three days, was thrown away on the second day, being quite uneatable.

Febry 7th. Moved on again at midnight, leading our horses as the bush was very thick and the path narrow. At daybreak I began to make my breakfast off some gum which I had broken from the mimosa tree, but it gave me such terrible pains in the jaws that I was soon glad to give up the job as hopeless; in fact, so much so that I never ventured to indulge in the luxury of a gum breakfast again.

Suddenly we came on two men, mounted on good horses, but, the bush being thick, their movements were very slow. Our meeting was so sudden and unexpected that they had no time to get away from us, so appeared to have come to the conclusion that they would try and bounce us out of their identity. The very novel mode adopted by the Officer of proving them of having been at some time soldiers, I shall not disclose. Suffice for me to say it took them by surprise, and so it would the most cute. These also were sent to the Prison at Sidbury.

After this little job we rested a few hours, then moved on again toward the nearest road out of the forest as we were sadly in want of food. This was the second day without a bit of anything to eat except gum—I must not forget that.

Just before dusk we came to a farm house and three of us went to try and get something to eat. The Officer had the power to compel owners to furnish us with food if he thought proper, but he did not want them to know what business we were on.

The owner, an Englishman, refused to let us have anything whatever unless he was compelled. He was of the true Colonial stamp—hated the very name of a soldier.

The Officer wanted for nothing;he had a pack horse well loaded with the good things of this life. But there is one thing I give him credit for—when he had any refreshment he did not tantalise us by taking it in front of us;he invariably hid himself from us in the bush.

As there was nothing to be got at the house, we returned to our party with long faces and empty stomachs. But "fortune invariably favours the brave." We caught sight of three goats grazing— belonging to the farm beyond a doubt. Whether they did or not was not much consequence to us who had been nearly three days without a particle of food. In less than one hour their throats were cut, their skins off, and their bones scattered over the ground, clean picked.

One of our party said,"Paddy, go up to the house and ax 'em to give you a pinch o' salt," but Paddy said he would make shift without the salt. I can well speak from long experience in bush living—any kind of meat,frizzled on the embers of a fire on the ground, is most insipid without a little salt.

After our meal,could we but have managed a whiff of the fragrant weed we should have been all right. As it was, we were obliged to console ourselves without, and double up under a bush for a few hours.

Febry 8th. Started at midnight for another Forest, *Long Kloof.* During the night we lost our guide. He told the Officer it was no use to go there, but the Officer decided to go. We might as well have staid away. Information had reached there before us.We came to a number of huts, but there was no one there but Hottentot women and children—the whole of them filthy in the extreme.The depravity in which men exist in those forests is beyond description.

As there was not the most remote chance of catching any more deserters, we began to make our way back to Graham's Town.At night we came to a farm house, and here we were supplied with a sheep, and one pound of flour for each man. By the time the sheep was killed and cut up, two large camp kettles were lent us to cook it in; and I have no doubt but there were others like myself, anxious to have a dip in the pot. At length the mutton was done and the cakes baked and the whole very soon put out of sight, after which we settled down for the night.

A drove of jackalls paid us a visit, who had, I make no doubt, scented our mutton from afar, but I am rather inclined to think there was very little more than bones came to their share.

Febry 9th. Moved on again at daylight, and at mid-day, being near some good pasturage, we off-saddled and let the horses graze for a few hours. In the evening we reached a small settlement—Church Place. We had scarcely dismounted when we were accosted by a portly old lady who invited the whole of us to her house to partake of what she could give us. We were not long in accepting the invite.

In a very short time a large camp kettle of tea was made, and a good supply of *Bel Tongue* and bread was set before us. The old lady told us that her present husband was a Dutchman. I had guessed that the moment I saw the *Bel Tong* as this kind of meat is seldom found in the houses of Englishmen. It is made from beef cut from the very best beast procurable, cut into long strips and dried. Her first husband was a Hospital Sergeant in the Royal Artillery. She told us:

"What you cannot eat take with you as you will not find another house between this and Graham's Town."

Having made a hearty meal, we were just thinking of getting back to our horses and making ourselves snug for the night when the husband of the good lady came home; and he very soon satisfied us as to his approval of his wife's conduct by producing a large calabash of brandy. The Officer joined us, and we had a right jolly night of it.

Febry 10th. Reached Graham's Town. A few days after the five men we had taken were tried and convicted of desertion. £15 was allowed, which was called "blood money," to be divided among the party, and each man received in addition ten shillings as extra field allowance.

I was only in Graham's Town a short time when I was sent with a small detachment to *Beka Kloof*. We encamped close to the Missionary Station and I had many opportunities of seeing what was going on—so much for my inquisitiveness.

Close to the Station there were a number of huts, occupied by Fingoes and a few Kaffirs, but the whole of them were the servants of the Missionary. The little bell at the Station rang for prayers at 9 a.m. and 6 p.m. while our Camp was there.

One evening I made bold to enter and join the congregation which consisted of five men, two of whom might have been Kaffirs, 9 women and several children. When the prayers were concluded which were conducted by one of the converts, I satisfied myself that there was not one present who was not a servant to the Missionary. During the short time we were in this Camp I visited the Station Chapel twice. On the day following my second visit the Missionary came to me and asked if I understood the Kaffir language. I said I did not when he informed me that I must not go into the Chapel any more; and he wanted to know what I had been writing down during my visit.

However, I did go again, but was refused admission. I asked for the Missionary, and was told by one of his servants that he had gone shooting.

A most singular coincidence occurred while in this Camp. I received a pamphlet from my brother in England in reference to Missionary labours in South Africa, principally among the Kaffirs, which had been published in England about ten months prior to my receiving it; and most prominent was an account of the "Wonderful Progress of Christianity among the Kaffirs in the vicinity of Beka Station." I will give one extract only from the pamphlet.

"The station bell rings for prayers at 9 a.m., also at 3p.m. and at 6 p.m. At the first sound of the bell the Kaffirs are seen leaving their cattle and rushing to the Chapel, which, being very small, is soon filled and many have to remain outside."

Where did the Kaffirs come from that came "rushing to the Chapel" when the bell rang? Anyone that had been in Kaffirland knows well how far this will go in truth. Any person reading the pamphlet—unacquainted with Kaffirland—would be led to believe that there were at least a dozen droves of cattle always near the Station, and as many herds to each drove.

Being on the spot, I could judge for myself. I never saw, during my stay there, one drove of cattle near the Station that did not belong to the Missionary or his servants. The Kaffirs knew too well what the consequence would be if a drove of their cattle should by accident stray anywhere near the Station. They would immediately be taken possession of by the servants of the Missionary and a certain number of them confiscated—and such confiscation was invariably approved of by the authorities.

A short time afterward I returned the pamphlet to my brother with the following written on the fly leaf:

"In reference to the account of the Beka Station herein, if things were as stated at the date of publication, which is barely twelve months back, they are very different now."

I do not wish it to be thought for one moment that I am in any way prejudiced against Missionaries. Very far from that as I have met some who have been most zealous and earnest in their profession, such as Mr. Moffatt of Fort Beaufort, Mr. Livingstone, Mr. Calderwood of Block Drift, Mr. Barnes—I believe that was his name—who had a Station at Fort Peddie, and several others whose names I do not now remember.

March 24th, '46. Returned to Graham's Town, and the following day was one of a detachment of 10 Dragoons and 25 of the 27th Regiment who were ordered to proceed to Cawood's Post.

Why called a Post I could not imagine, as there was no kind of Barrack there—only a very dilapidated farm house, but I believe the place had been used during a former Kaffir war, a number of Troops having been stationed there for the purpose of keeping open communications between Graham's Town and the Great Fish River.

The farm had been occupied by Mr. Cawood, but previous to our arrival it had been empty for some time. There was also another house occupied by the Commissariat Issuer, Mr. Regan. This house, small as it was, also contained the Commissariat Stores, for the protection of which we had been sent. The said stores consisted of a few bags of biscuits very old and mouldy. Mr. Regan said the last time he examined the biscuit—about two years since—he did not think anyone could eat it. There were also a few barrells of "salt junk." The number of years these stores had been there was unknown. Mr. Regan said he had taken over the junk when he first came there, about nine years ago.

I had nearly omitted to mention that among the stores outside the house was a stack of oat straw. This was the kind of Commissariat Stores in those times.

It now became very evident that the Kaffirs were preparing for war. Great signal fires were burning every night on the Amatola Mountains, the great stronghold of the Gaika Tribes.

April 1st, '46. The ten Dragoons of this detachment were ordered to return to Graham's Town, where every preparation was being made for war. Only 12 years had elapsed since the last war, and nearly the same time between the two previous wars—and now on the eve of another.

April 3rd, '46. Two waggon loads of ammunition were sent from Graham's Town, under the escort of 40 men of the 27th Regiment, en route for Fort Beaufort. At midnight a report reached us that the Kaffirs had come down, murdered the escort, and carried off the whole of the ammunition.

I was one of 25 Dragoons ordered to saddle up and start immediately for Fort Brown. We reached the Fort at daylight, having galloped nearly the whole distance, 24 miles. The report was found to be without foundation. The escort had not seen a Kaffir up to the time they arrived at this Post, and had gone on to Fort Beaufort.

The extensive Commissariat Stores of this noted Fort, which was only 24 miles from Graham's Town, the largest town on the Frontiers, within two days of a declaration of war—which was to last two years—could not furnish us with a feed of corn for our horses. As there was no forage to be had from the Stores, it was no use staying there so we went off to Koonap.

There was an African hotel there, where we obtained fodder for our horses, but we should have got nothing for ourselves but for the kindness of the Officer in command, who gave to each man what ever he could purchase to the value of one shilling. So soon as the proprietor knew this, he doubled the price of every article he proposed to dispose of to us. Each man received a few biscuits and half a pint of common wine; value of the whole about twopence.

In the evening a heavy thunderstorm came on, and this specimen of the English Colonist actually refused us shelter, even to use one of his numerous sheds. He said he would as soon have a lot of Kaffirs about his house as Soldiers. He little thought then that before two months were past he would be very glad to creep to the side of one of them for protection. I must not omit this gentleman's name; it was Jackson.

As we could not get any place for shelter and the horses having had rest and a feed, the Officer—although he had good quarters in the Hotel—would not stop there while his men had to stand exposed to the heavy rain, so he decided to return to Graham's Town.

Chapter Ten
War with the Gaika Tribes

April, '46. War was declared against the whole of the Gaika Tribes.

When I relate the cause of this war, which lasted nearly two years and lost England over 3 millions of money besides the sacrifice of human life, I think there will be some who will scarcely credit it and will laugh at the idea. Still, the facts are well known.

A Kaffir of the Gaika tribe, under that portion that was ruled by Maccomo, had stolen an old chopper—valued 4d.—the property of the Ordnance Department. The thief was traced to his kraal and the chopper found in his possession within the territory of the Chief Maccomo, who, on application, gave over the thief to the British Authorities for punishment. The case having been investigated at Fort Beaufort, the thief was committed to take his trial at Graham's Town, to which place he was on his way with two other prisoners, an Englishman and a Hottentot, the whole of them under the escort of 12 men of the 91st Regiment. The Hottentot was handcuffed to the Kaffir, and I believe the English man was handcuffed by himself.

They had not proceeded far from the Fort when, in passing through a ravine known as Mildenhall's Kloof—the name of the proprietor of a farm that was situated within 200 yards—a great number of Kaffirs variously estimated at from one to two thousand rushed upon the escort; and before the latter had time to load poor old "Brown Bess," they were overpowered by the Kaffirs, who took possession of the prisoners and made off.

They were determined to release their countryman, but could not unfasten the handcuffs. The only way to accomplish their object was to cut off the hand of the Hottentot, and this they did with an assegaie. They then made off for the bush, leaving the Englishman and the Hottentot to rejoin the escort, the latter minus one hand.

The escort returned to the Fort and a squadron of Dragoons was ordered in pursuit, but the Kaffirs got clear away with the thief.

Application was then made to the Paramount Chief, Sandilla, by the Authorities for the surrender of the prisoner and all who were engaged in the rescue. Sandilla refused to comply, so there was no alternative but to declare war, which was done. Had a slight castigation been administered to the thief in the first instance, what sacrifice of life might have been prevented, and no less a sum than 3 millions been saved to England besides the disgrace of more than one defeat by naked Kaffirs.

On the same day that war was declared I was appointed one of the bodyguard of the General, Sir Peregrine Maitland, and ordered to Post Victoria.

April 7th, '46. The General and his Staff went out reconnoitering and were accompanied for a short distance by Captain Sandes of the Cape Mounted Rifles, who, with an escort of six men of the same Regiment, was on his way to Block Drift to join the Head Quarters of his Regiment.

When Captain Sandes left us he had about five miles to go, but neither him nor his escort ever reached their destination. They were waylaid on the road, which went through a dense bush, and the whole were killed or fell into the hands of the Kaffirs. The skeleton of Captain Sandes was discovered some months after, a considerable distance from any part of his route, on the Debe Flats. His remains were identified by his card and spectacle case which were found near the remains, also a portion of his clothing. It is supposed that he alone was taken prisoner and brought to this place and then put to a lingering death.

April 8th. I was one of a party of 12 Dragoons and 25 of the 27th Regiment who were ordered to patrol round the outskirts of the Post (Victoria) but having gone farther than we should have done, we had the misfortune to get into a deep ravine, and before we could extricate ourselves we were surrounded by Kaffirs. All were armed with assegaies—long spear with blade barbed like a fish hook—-and some in addition had guns. There was a straggling bush, and this prevented them from using the assegaie.

They gathered around us like a lot of bees. I shot three of them, one after another, as fast as I could load. The order was given to make our way out of the ravine as quick as we could. The thick bush prevented us from going any faster than the horses could walk. The Dragoons were all dismounted and leading their horses. Once or twice I heard a dispute between the Officer in command of the Infantry and the one who commanded the Dragoons, the former saying several times: "I beg your pardon, Captain Hogg, but it is the place of the Dragoons to cover the retreat of my men."

Yes, he was quite right if the Dragoons had been mounted. But, being on foot, placed us on a par with the Infantry in one sense, but in reality much worse because we had our horses to look after as well as ourselves.

The Kaffirs were yelling like a lot of furies. I noticed those who had guns discharged them from the hip and not from the shoulder. They had no knowledge of the quantity of powder required, putting it out of the horn slung over their shoulder into the hand, and from thence to barrel. A table spoonful more or less did not appear of much consequence. The result was the old guns kicked and knocked them down. Fortunately, we had plenty of ammunition. A great number of the enemy must have fallen, they were so near us, yet they came madly on.

The Infantry were much worse off than we, as they were loaded with greatcoat and blanket on their backs, and 120 rounds of ball cartridge. What they wanted with a greatcoat and blanket, I could not imagine. Perhaps it was thought that the men would like to sleep before they returned. I know that several Officers of the distinguished Regiment to which I had the honour of belonging looked on the commencement of this war as the beginning of a glorious succession of picnic parties.

We were obliged to lead our horses and blaze away as hard as we could. A Sergeant of the 27th—Mellon—was shot through the left ankle and fell to the ground, saying, "For God's sake, comrades, don't leave me behind!"

I stopped, with two others of his own Regiment, and raised him up. One of those two was shot while holding the Sergeant; I believe he was a Corporal. I and the other man tried to raise the Sergeant on to my horse, but could not, he was so heavy. The poor fellow could not throw his leg over the saddle, and Spider would not stand still. We shouted for help, but the noise was so great we could not be heard. Everyone was making his way up the hill, entirely ignorant of the position we were in.

At length we were obliged to drop him and at that moment a Kaffir drove the muzzle of his gun right into the poor fellow's body. The other man (who was helping me) must have been shot dead as I do not remember seeing him after he fell. Both bodies fell into the hands of the Kaffirs. I was struck on the left shoulder by a spent ball before I reached the top of the hill.

The firing having been heard from the Post, a reinforcement was sent to us and after a few volleys we drove the enemy off and made an attempt to recover the wounded, but did not succeed. They had been dragged away by the Kaffirs. We reached Victoria at sunset.

What I witnessed that day baffles description. I really believe I shot 20 Kaffirs myself.

But our day's work was not yet over. The time for our cattle to be brought in for the night had passed and they had not arrived, nor was there any sign of them coming over the hills which surrounded the Post. At length the herds came running in and reported that the Kaffirs had driven off the whole of our cattle in the direction of Fish River.

The general opinion was that the herds had allowed the Kaffirs to drive off the cattle without attempting the slightest resistance or even giving any alarm until the Kaffirs had got well out of the way with their booty. But at that time I don't think there was any sympathy between the Kaffirs and the Fingo herds.—The proper name, of the latter, I believe, is "Fingis," which in the Kaffir language signifies "slave."— These people were also Kaffirs and at one time a very powerful Tribe, but were at length overpowered by a number of Tribes united and they were made slaves of the victors. The Tribe was broken up and scattered among the various Tribes engaged who had conquered them, and in order that they might be known, a hole was cut in the lobe of each ear, and every child born of them was marked in a similar manner.

20 Dragoons and 40 Cape Mounted Rifles were sent off in pursuit of the cattle, and we were very near falling into a trap. The moon was shining very bright; we could see the Kaffirs driving a few of the cattle a short distance in front of us, but these were so few it was not thought worth while to go after them.

Shortly after, in another direction, there were about 50 oxen driven just over the hill in order that we might see them. There was a deep kloof or ravine between us and the cattle. The Officer in Command did not like the look of our position and sent a Hottentot Private of the Cape Mounted Rifles, dismounted, down the kloof to ascertain if there were any Kaffirs there. The Totty never returned. Quite evidently he fell into the trap. We then returned to the Post, reaching it at daybreak, and within one hour the hills as far as the eye could reach were covered with Kaffirs. They had got the whole of our Commissariat and draft cattle, about 400, and had divided them in three droves, each of which they repeatedly drove over the brow of the hill, defying the Troops to go out and take them.

The number of Kaffirs was estimated at sixty thousand, while the whole of our Force did not exceed 600 men of all ranks, which was entirely useless against such odds as that. Several times during the day the Kaffir came down and attacked us on all sides,and each time were driven back with great loss.They were mown down like grass by the grape and shell of our Artillery.

Captain Shepherd —the deaf Officer—had command of the Artillery and several times he elevated the guns himself and made some wonderful shots. He sent two 24 lb. shells right into the centre of about 4,000 Kaffirs.He certainly was a most experienced artillerist, but, without exception, the greatest tyrant I ever met in the Service.

Just before sunset, at the close of the last attack, a number of Dragoons and Cape Mounted Rifles, well covered by Artillery, made a dash after one lot of cattle and succeeded in retaking 94 of our draft oxen. The whole of the Troops remained under arms during the night, the Kaffirs giving us a few shots now and then as a shell was thrown among them for their amusement.

As the Kaffirs did not trouble us the following day, it was devoted to clearing away the dead from the immediate vicinity of the Post.The party of which I was one, buried during the day in one kloof 226 bodies, and we could see where hundreds of others had been dragged away during the past night. We did not find one with a sign of life in him.

April 14, '46. I joined the 1st or right division of the Army in the Field under Colonel Somerset.

April 15th. A great number of cattle having been seen passing over a ridge within sight of our Camp, a party of Dragoons and Cape Mounted Rifles were ordered off in pursuit under the command of Captain Bambrick, 7th Dragoon Guards.

They had not proceeded far when they perceived the enemy approaching on all sides. The cattle had only been driven over the ridge as a decoy.The Officer gave the order for the Troops to retire a short distance as the bush was too thick for the movements of mounted men and I have no doubt intended to get on more open ground, thinking perhaps he might induce the enemy to come somewhat more into the open.

He had scarcely given the order when he was shot and fell head foremost over the front of the saddle. He must have been shot through the heart, as he never spoke after. An attempt was made to recover the body, but they were not successful. The bush was too thick and the number of the enemy was increasing, and the party thought it advisable to return to Camp.

The horse of the deceased Officer made his way back to the Camp, and the quantity of blood found on the front part of the saddle and down the horse's shoulder confirmed the opinion before expressed that he had been shot through the heart.

A strong party of Dragoons and Cape Mounted Rifles was sent out to endeavour to recover the body. They found the place where he had fallen, and saw also where the body had been dragged along the grass. The trail was followed to a considerable distance, but was eventually lost in the thick bush.

In this Officer, I lost the best friend I ever had in the Service. Some time after his death I was told by Major Sir Harry Darell that Captain Bambrick had left me £300— such he had heard—also that the Captain had left a will which had been made only a few days previous to his death. However I never got anything. In his private memorandum book was an entry dated 17th December, 1845:

"I have made up my mind to go home next spring, and as I have taken a great liking to that boy, I shall take him with me."

The entry in reference to the watch I was to have was also found, but a pen with ink had been drawn through it. Again there was one without date:

"I am pleased to hear such a good account of that boy. I have set aside £50 for him."

As all this was only hearsay, I could not vouch for it being correct. However, I made application to the Commanding Officer of the Regiment in reference to the matter and was informed that the deceased Officer's effects had been sold and the proceeds of his estate sent to the War Office, to which I was directed to apply for any further information I wanted on the subject.

But I did not trouble further about it. The Captain had told me several times that he had a daughter living at Windsor, to whom I should have written had I known her address, not with the idea of getting the money—I did not want that—but I should have liked to have had some little article as a memento. Robert Bambrick, Rest in Peace.

Very shortly after this happened the Right Division of the Army lost the whole of their baggage train and stores (at Burns Hill) contained in 96 waggons consisting of camp equipage and the whole of the Office Books belonging to the 7th Dragoon Guards. Why the books had been brought into the Field I could not imagine. The Officers' Mess plate, which they had brought with them in anticipation of the splendid picnics they intended giving, the whole of the Dragoons' necessaries and valises, which only that very morning had been removed from the saddles in order to make them lighter for the horses, and placed in the waggons, two waggons containing veterinary and hospital stores, two waggons loaded with wines belonging to the Officers, and two loaded with ammunition. Part of the latter was saved but with this exception the whole was lost in the bush at Burns Hill.

The Officer in Command, having reason to believe the enemy was farther from us than they proved to be, had left his stores on the road in a thick bush with a bodyguard of only 50 men. The Baggage Train extended over five miles, thus leaving only one man to guard two waggons, occupying a distance of 176 yards. The number of the enemy was unknown. Had destruction of life been their only object, they could easily have killed every man of the guard in detail.

Plunder was their object, and they had it very comfortable with little annoyance.

But what a contrast! A few months back we were plundering the Dutch farm houses. Yes, we were plundering the deserted homesteads of the Dutch Boers. Now the bold Dragoons were being plundered of the wines, plate, stores, etc., by a lot of naked Kaffirs in front of their very faces— not a creditable contrast by any means.

It happened entirely by chance that the two waggons containing the ammunition were the first two of the train, and by hard fighting a considerable portion of it was saved.

Eventually the Baggage Guard, with their wounded, reached Block Drift Missionary Station; and the Division arrived shortly afterward minus the whole of its stores, camp equipage, etc. The wounded were placed in the deserted Missionary Station. By the by, what had become of all the converts? Gone to convert their brethren, I make no doubt.

The Division stood under arms the whole night— not a tent to cover us or a morsel of food to eat, the rain coming down in lumps the whole of the night and shot flying about like hailstones. This was indeed a pleasant prospect for the commencement of a war that was to last nearly two years; and not the shadow of a chance of getting one particle of clothing, tents, cooking utensils or anything else for the next six months.

The following morning the Division started to go over the ground traversed by the Baggage train the day previous. The remains of the first waggon we came to had been loaded with horse medicine. We found several bodies near it, blown out like bladders. They had been searching for the *umlelah manza*—firewater—and had found something much stronger than they bargained for.

Every wagon along the whole line had been plundered and then set on fire. The draft oxen numbering near one thousand were clean gone. The bush was strewn with fragments of clothing, from which every particle of gold lace or brass button had disappeared. The whole of the wine and plate belonging to the Officers and the whole of the Office Books were destroyed—much to the gratification of some whose names were transcribed therein for deeds which do not in general precede promotion.

A Kaffir was seen sitting near the remains of one of the waggons, but on getting near he was found to be dead. He had no marks about him, so I concluded he had been poisoned. As there was not one single article to be seen that was worth the trouble of carrying, we returned to Block Drift.

Chapter Eleven
Infiltrating Our Lines

April 21st, 1846. In consequence of the number of horses wounded during the past two nights by stray shots from the Kaffirs, and several having been stolen from the outskirts of the Camp and one man badly wounded last night while on sentry, an order was issued that all sentries on the outer lines of the Camp were to lie flat on the belly. This was done in order that we might have as good a chance as the Kaffirs, as it was well known that their mode of approaching their object at night time was on their belly, balancing the body on the hands and toes, and their gun slung across their back.

This order was found to answer remarkably well as the following, morning four Kaffirs were found dead on the outer lines, having been shot by the Sentries, also one fellow who was still alive. He had been shot at the back of the leg at the bend of the knee, the muscles of which were severed as though cut with a knife. I assisted to carry him to an empty hut near at hand, and left him in charge of some Hottentots while I went to inform the Surgeon, but on my return with the Doctor the fellow was beyond cure. The Hottentots—then the Kaffirs' most bitter enemies—had set fire to the hut, and the Kaffir had been burned to death.

April 23rd, '46. During the past night, when on sentry on the outer line, I was laying flat on the ground with my gun loaded and capped, the rain coming down very heavy, when suddenly I saw something moving in front of me. The night was very dark. I signalled to the next Sentry, who was only 20 yards from me and proved to be my old particular friend with the hairy face. He also could see some object in front, and he said in a low tone of voice:

"Have a shot at him, Buck."

Still I was determined to reserve my fire until the object came nearer. I had no fear of missing as at this time I was considered one of the best shots in the Regiment. I had made myself efficient by always making it a practice never to throw away a round of ammunition without having something for it. The Sentries on the outer lines were not allowed to challenge as no one went beyond them after dark.

The object kept moving, and I imagined moving away from me and, being fearful that I might lose a chance for a shot, I fired and soon found out that I had shot a horse instead of a Kaffir as the poor beast came hopping towards me on three legs.

The following morning I was taken before the Commanding Officer for shooting a horse belonging to the Commissariat Officer. When the case was investigated I received great credit for my vigilance, more especially as the night was dark and it was raining hard at the time; and the Commissariat Officer was directed to have his horse more securely fastened at night in future. My shot had grazed the near fore leg and passed through the hock of the off hind leg; the horse had to be killed.

April 25th, '46. Our Division moved from Block Drift for the purpose of patrolling the dense kloofs of the Kowie Bush. On arrival at the Kowie, we took possession of a deserted farm house which had been occupied by a Scotch farmer named McClucky, but (he) had left it when the war began. Colonel Somerset would not allow us to occupy the house; we had to bivouac in the bush adjacent. We had no camp equipment whatever, not even a camp kettle to boil meat.

It was here that we got the first taste of that cruel mismanagement which followed us for the next 18 months. We were within 30 miles of Graham's Town, the largest town on the Frontiers of the Cape of Good Hope—"The Garden of Eden," as the Recruiting Sergeant told me when I enlisted, but I was of opinion that if it was so, it was a place that was very scantily provided with provisions. The Troops comprising this, the 1st or Right Division of the Army were actually subsisting on 8 ounces of dirty wheat per day which had been found in the house when we took possession.

Most of the Officers fared no better than the Privates, the same allowance of wheat,the same shelter, the Canopy of Heaven.

Each night as soon as darkness set in the Kaffirs began,and kept up, a continuous fire until daybreak. All Sentries were doubled—two men in place of one—and to lay on the ground, all fires out at dusk, and rain every night—not a pleasant position to be in, laying on the wet ground face downward for two hours, cold and wet, one's head going right and left like the pendulum of a clock, watching every opportunity for a shot in front.

One morning the Kaffirs came down toward us in three Divisions, and every preparation was made to give them a warm reception. The Artillery was well concealed in the bush. Our horses were always kept saddled from sunrise to sunset. The Kaffirs advanced very slowly but kept shouting to us to come out.

The Dragoons and Cape Mounted Rifles were divided into three parties.As we had four guns,two were told off for one party who were about attacking the greatest body of the enemy, and one gun each to the other two.

By this time the Kaffirs were within 100 yards of us. At length the order was given and out we rushed.I was with the party that had two guns. I never saw the Artillery make such practice. Each round cut a complete road through the mass of Kaffirs in front of us.The Dragoons and Cape Mounted Rifles fired away as hard as they were able. The Kaffirs made only a short stand, then broke and fled.

The order was then given:"Dragoons to the front. Draw swords. Gallop. Charge!"

Several of the Artillery joined in the charge, and if the reception the Kaffirs met with was not quite as warm as they expected, it was not our fault. As the whole of them were armed no mercy was shown them, nor did they ask for it.

The same day I was one of a party of 10 Dragoons and 30 Cape Mounted Rifles, under the command of Captain Hogg, 7th Dragoon Guards, that was ordered to Theopolis— a Missionary Station about 18 miles distant—with two barrels of ammunition.

When we reached there we found it was a Hottentot Settlement as well as a Missionary Station. The Missionary had left for Graham's Town when the war broke out. In fact they all done the same, and wise they were in so doing as the Kaffirs had no mercy on any white man who fell into their hands.

The Hottentots at the Settlement had plenty of guns but no ammunition. All they wanted was plenty of the latter and they had no fear of the Kaffirs. Captain Hogg was instructed to tell them that they would need to be very careful with what we had brought as it was impossible to say when they would get any more—not for some time to come, at all events.

We then began to look about for something to eat, and caught sight of a cow grazing a short distance off. Half a dozen of us started to bring her in, fortunately not without our arms. We got within 30 yards of her when several shots were fired from a clump of bush close by. The cow was evidently there as a decoy. But hungry men were not to be frightened at trifles, and as none of us had been the recipient of a pill we made a dash toward her, when a number of Kaffirs rushed from the bush. We fired, and five out of six shots took effect as that number of Kaffirs were found to be either killed or winged. They threw several assegaies at us and two of our party were wounded, but before the Kaffirs got clear of us two more of their number fell.

One of our party was wounded in the arm, the other through the shoulder. The latter was a very nasty wound caused by a barbed assegaie; and as the blade, like a fishhook, could not be drawn back, the whole length of the assegaie shaft had to be drawn through the poor fellow's shoulder, which was a very painful operation as well as tedious, as it was necessary to be very careful in cleaning the shaft as much as possible in order that no dirt might pass from it into the wound.

We brought in the cow, and in a very short time lumps of her flesh were frizzling on the fires which had been prepared for the purpose. What would we not have given for the luxury of a pinch of salt or even a "*Rodney*" ration of biscuit! But we had been strangers to such dainties for a considerable time past. For what we had, such as it was, we were thankful.

The following morning we saw a large quantity of poultry running about that appeared to have no owner. So we thought we might as well have a portion as to leave them there for the Kaffirs to take away, as it was quite evident that the Totties would not remain on the Station long after we left, as there was already some dispute among them in reference to the division of the ammunition we had brought them.

I was speaking to one of them—by this time I was able to converse in the Dutch language and was also making fair progress in the Kaffir language—a Hottentot, who told me the majority of them at the Station had made up their mind to go to Graham's Town, as they had heard that a Hottentot Levy was about to be raised there and they should go and join it as they would get good pay.

We did not ask permission of the Officer to seize the poultry as we did not think it worth while. We began operations, and in a few minutes had knocked over about thirty of different sorts. The horse that had brought the ammunition was soon loaded with as many as we could fasten on the pack saddle, all of us being under the impression that the poultry would be equally divided on our reaching the Camp.

We had not proceeded far on our return journey—not more than four miles—when, in passing through a bush, The Kaffirs opened fire on us. And we had no chance to return the compliment, the bush being so very thick, so we acted the wisest plan under the circumstances by clapping spurs to our horses and getting through the bush as fast as we could.

We had the two wounded men with us. One of them was getting on well, but the man who was wounded through the shoulder was in great pain. Before we cleared the bush we had one horse killed and one man with his thighbone smashed with a piece of chain link which had been fired at him.

We had great difficulty in getting him along. The poor fellow was not able to sit on the horse any way. He was in great agony. At length we were obliged to make a kind of litter with some branches of trees covered with the soft branches of the wild tea tree. There was no ambulances or Army Service Corps. If the wounded man could not sit on a horse or bear to be carried on the crossed hands of two men, it would be very probable that the following day he would be beyond trouble; perhaps returned as "missing." We were determined not to leave him behind while there was half a chance of saving him, knowing well what his fate would be if he fell into the hands of the Kaffirs. Fortunately, they had ceased firing at us directly after the man was wounded. They had not seen it; if they had they would not have left us as they did. As it was, the poor fellow died just before we reached the Camp.

With regard to the poultry, we were much out in our calculations. They were coolly taken possession of by the Officers and divided among themselves, except one very old turkey which none care to accept and was flung aside. My chum asked Captain Hogg if he might have the rejected turkey.

"Yes," said the Captain, "you may have him if you can make any use of him."

My chum took possession of him, and such a bunch of bones and feathers I never saw. However, he was soon stripped of the latter, and the former in four pieces was frizzling on the fire. I have no doubt but there was more attention bestowed on his body now than there ever had been during life. At length he was done and "to a turn" as a matter of course. My chum asked me if I should like a pinch of salt.

"No such luck," said I.

"Try that," said he, at the same time sprinkling something over the piece I held in my fingers. "Well, what do you think of it?"

"It certainly is salt to the taste, yet I cannot say that I admire it,"

My chum expressed his own opinion several times by saying "capital substitute," but I would have preferred my portion of turkey without the substitute. If the tough old chap had not filled our bellies, at least he had given us the jaws ache.

As the substitute in question had left a very peculiar taste in my mouth, I was anxious to know of what it consisted. I asked my comrade where he got it from, and the following was the account he gave me:

"While you were sitting by the fire cooking the turkey, I saw Doctor Walsh of the Royal Artillery throw away the head and backbone of a red herring; and, knowing well from what little I have tasted of those fish sent out from England (how salt they are) I thought I would try an experiment. So I roasted the head and bone by the fire and then rubbed them into powder—and I'll never want salt again so long as I can get the head and backbone of a red herring."

About three miles from our Camp there was a very large farm occupied by an Englishman. His name was Dell. He was the greatest contractor for horse forage in the Colony. A few days since he had an immense stock on hand. It was reported in the Camp that an offer for the whole of his stock of forage had been made by the Commissariat Officer which Mr. Dell had refused to accept.

However, this morning at daybreak he and his wife and family reached our Camp. The Kaffirs had set fire to the whole of his property, and they barely had time to escape with their lives. Twice since we had been in this Camp Colonel Somerset had advised him to sell his stock and abandon the place, but Mr. Dell said he felt satisfied the Kaffirs would not molest him or his family He employed nearly all Kaffirs about his farm, and had been told by them that he or his farm would never be interfered with during the war unless other tribes joined them, in which case he would receive timely notice.

But they deceived him. The warning, he got this morning was from a Hottentot servant who overheard the Kaffirs saying that a portion of their Tribe was coming down to destroy the place, but would not attack Mr. Dell or his family if he did not fire upon them. But if he did fire on them they would kill him and the whole of his family. Thus it is in this beautiful country, a man may be comparatively wealthy today, a beggar tomorrow.

Directly after the arrival of Mr. Dell and his family. a party consisting, of Artillery, Dragoons and C.M.Rifles was sent to Dell's farm in pursuit of the enemy. Directly we came in sight of the place we could see a great number of Kaffirs, but all disappeared in the bush as we approached. The cattle had been driven off, and the farm and the whole of the stock destroyed. Exposure to all weathers and insufficiency of food began to tell on the biggest and strongest looking men. Dysentery was very bad, more particularly among the biggest men. As to myself, I never had better health in my life. I could never content myself to sit idle; must be doing something even if it was mischief or that which I should not do. The big fellows used to say of me: "Oh, no sickness will ever come on that fellow; there's nothing of him."

The Kaffirs kept us moving night and day. At night they kept up a constant fire on our Bivouac and at day time they continually showed themselves over the brow of the hills surrounding our Bivouac. But always they took care to clear off as soon as we turned out to go after them. They had not forgotten the dressing they got a short time previous.

One day Captain Hogg, 7th Dragoon Guards, sent his servant to Colonel Somerset—with whom he was most intimate—with his compliments to ask if he could spare anything from his scanty store, as Capt. Hogg could not possibly make use of the wheat.

Colonel Somerset returned his compliments with all he could spare, namely one red herring.

Chapter Twelve
Ambush on the Convoy

April 27th, 1846. Two waggonloads of biscuit reached us from Graham's Town, and by its antique appearance many were of opinion that it was a portion of that which had been left by the Dutch when they surrendered the Cape to the English. Being nearly as hard as flint stones, it was almost necessary that each man should be supplied with a hammer in order that he might bruise the biscuit before handing it over to the jaw department. I don't know how the poor old fellows got on whose teeth were like mine now—very bad. And the meat was bad in the extreme. A lot of sheep had been sent to us from Graham's Town. They were nothing but skin and bones; in fact, had one of them been hung up and a candle placed inside it would have answered very well for a lantern. There was no beef to be had as the Kaffirs had driven away all the beasts fit for killing; in fact, they left none whatever.

May 29th, '46. The Kaffirs paid us a visit twice during the past night. They shouted to us that they had plenty of cattle and dared us to come out and take them. But they made a mistake. We did go out, but got no cattle as they had none with them. We exchanged a few shots, but because it was very dark we could not see our way to go far after them. this morning we found four of them who had been shot very close up to our Camp. Strange they had not been dragged away during the night.

When the baggage train was lost at Burns Hill the Officers of the 7th Dragoon Guards lost a very large quantity of wine which, according to the writing of some poetical wag in the Graham's Town Journal, was carried away by Maccomo's Tribe into the Amatola Mountains. The following is a copy:

"*Maccomo, Kaffir Chief, to Messrs. Bell,
Rennie & Co., Wine Merchants,
Edinburgh.*

Gentlemen:

*Having lately drank some sherry
Which really was delicious, very
The same as near as I can guess
You furnish to the Seventh Mess,
And finding in the Amatola
Good sherry is the best consola,
I request that you will send me
And 'twill very much befriend me
A pipe or two of the same wine,
A liquor truly most divine.
I've now drank all was in the waggons
We lately captured from the Draggons,
And though I feel quite loath to spare it
I fear shall have to broach the claret.
This order therefore pray fulfill
And with it send at once your bill.
A draft on some good house at Home-o*

*You'll quickly receive
From yours,*

Maccomo."

Who the author was is now a matter of indifference. Suffice it for the present, I knew him well.

May 30th, '46. Our Division was ordered to escort a convoy of 104 waggons laden with stores, provisions and ammunition, en route from Graham's Town to Fort Peddie; the Troops in the latter Fort having been reported in a state of starvation. This night we halted on the bank of the Committjees River. The rain fell heavy during the night. Not a tent to cover us; and the Kaffirs kept up an incessant fire on us the whole of the night.

May 31st. The advance guard moved on at daybreak; and long before the rear guard had moved, the former were attacked. The road, barely wide enough to admit of a waggon passing, lay through a dense bush, which was lined by thousands of the enemy.

The shot flew about like hail. Had but one thousandth part of their shots been effective, not one man of that Division would have seen another day. One minute the order would be given, "Send more men to the front!" The next it would be: "Reinforcements are wanted in the rear!"

We were obliged to halt every 10 or 20 yards to drag a dead or wounded bullock to one side of the road. The waggon oxen appeared nearly mad. They kept rushing into the bush, first on one side then on the other; and so near were the Kaffirs that they drove their assegaies into the bullocks from the bush at the roadside.

Our Force, which consisted of Cavalry and Artillery, were all dismounted, one man leading five or six horses and the remainder firing away as hard as they were able. I saw a Totty shot just in front of me. So close was the Kaffir who shot him that the muzzle or his gun struck the Totty on the cheek before the Kaffir discharged it. The charge was sufficient to blow part of the Totty's head off and knock down the Kaffir who fired it. He never fired another shot after that.

So numerous were the enemy that any man who could hit a house at 20 yards could not miss them. I do not wish to boast or exaggerate, but I declare that of 12 shots I fired in as quick succession as possible, I firmly believe that I brought down a Kaffir with every shot. How many narrow escapes I had I cannot say, but this I do know: I had a ball through my forage cap and I also know it must have been very close to my head. Every foot of ground was hard fought for. I saw a little Hottentot forelooper shot through both thighs. I caught him up and put the little fellow into one of the waggons. A short time after I came near the same waggon and the poor little Totty was dead.

It was near sunset when we reached the summit of the Committjees Mountain, having been 11 hours making a distance of less than nine miles. We suffered most terribly from thirst, which was accelerated by biting off the ends of the cartridges, which contained such a quantity of saltpetre.

It was midnight before the rear guard came up, but we had not lost a single waggon. We had only one or two killed and a few wounded, but we lost about five hundred of our draft oxen. When all had reached the summit, the waggons were put in a circle and the whole of the oxen and Artillery guns in the centre. Every soldier on field service at this time carried a small water barrel called a "calabash," and would hold about three pints of water. Some of the men, when passing through the river in the morning, had the good sense to fill their calabash; but, like many articles furnished for the use of the Soldier on field service, many of them were utterly useless for the purpose they were intended. They were so badly made they would not hold any water. Any man was well worthy of the name of "martyr" who carried one of those little implements of torture on his shoulder for one good day's march, and more especially if he had anything to do in the fighting line during his day's march.

Thus there were very few of us who could boast of having even a small portion of that essential beverage and many had none whatever. Not one of the Officers had a drop. It could not reasonably be expected that they would carry a calabash of water on their back the whole day. Five shillings were offered by several of them for only one dram of water; and if Major John Charles Hope Gibson is still alive I have no doubt he well remembers that night when he offered me one sovereign for half a pint of water. I could not spare that quantity, but gave him half of what I had, which was not more than half a pint altogether and my comrade had none, as his calabash was one of the useless ones. I don't think there was one of the Officers who met with a refusal from those who were fortunate enough to have any.

There is one thing I must relate which perhaps you will say was not very creditable. During the night I heard a Sergeant of the Artillery begging very hard of a Hottentot waggon driver for a drink of water. The Totty declared—nay, swore—that he had not a drop. I knew he had at least a gallon in his waggon barrel. I had seen it as I was laying under his waggon; and I also knew he had some coffee, as I saw him make it when the Sergeant went away. I followed him a few yards, then called to him, when I said:

"Sergeant Evans, you want some water and you shall have some. Come to the other side of that waggon. Keep your eye on me and you shall have water enough for a dozen of you."

He did so and had not long to wait. The Totty had filled his belly and, like the pigs, he laid himself down and went to sleep. I watched my opportunity and, creeping stealthily along, got hold of the barrel. My fingers touched a piece of string which was fastened to the barrel, at one end, and the other end of the string was tied around his wrist. With my knife I severed the string and carefully rolled the barrel to the Sergeant and told him to let me have it back again when he had emptied it. He did so, and I placed the empty barrel near the Totty's head.

I have said before, the waggons were placed in a circle, which was made as small as possible—in fact a great deal too small as the horses and bullocks were falling over each other—and all the Troops took up their quarters beneath the waggons. Every man was on the alert and the Kaffirs knew it. Still they gave us a few shots, but, the moon being up, they paid for it, as there was very little bush to cover them.

Shortly before daylight another waggon driver came and roused the sleeping Totty and asked if he was going to make any coffee before starting.

"If you do," said he, "make me about a pint as I have no water."

The selfish Totty replied: "I shan't make any. Have no water."

This time he spoke the truth although he was not aware of it. I had just previously fastened the ends of the string which I had severed. At the moment when he said he had no water he gave the string a tug and, finding the barrel there, he went off to sleep again. But not for long. He roused himself shortly after, set fire to a few sticks under the front of his waggon, then came with his little pot for water.

As I lay under the rear of the same waggon I could see the horrible look of the Totty when he discovered his loss. He rushed off to the driver who had visited him and found him with a pot of coffee on the ground before him, which the Totty instantly kicked over with his foot. A fight ensued, and the Totty came back with his nose bleeding. He never dreamt for one moment that the thief was lying so close to him all the time. He never even questioned me as to whether or not I had seen the theft committed.

June 1st, '46. At daylight the waggons were got ready for moving. We found that our loss of draft bullocks was much greater than w as expected; and it was quite evident that if we lost any more we should have to abandon some of our waggons. As it was, we divided them as best we could, and then made a start for Fort Peddie.

At the bottom of the mountain we had to pass through a small bush, and here the Kaffirs made a last and feeble attack. I saw a Kaffir place the barrel of his gun on the branch of a tree.—This he had no doubt learned from the Dutch, who invariably rest the gun on the saddle of their horse when taking aim at a distant object.—It was quite evident to me that he was selecting an Officer of the Cape Mounted Rifles as the object of his most particular attention. But he waited too long taking aim. I put a ball through his head and then divested him of his body adornments.

The firing having been heard from the Fort Peddie, the Dragoons were sent from thence to our assistance; and when they found we had brought provisions for the Troops stationed at the Fort, they gave us a hearty cheer. They had been for the last ten days subsisting on 6 ounces of salt junk per day;no biscuit,meal,tea,coffee or vegetable of any kind.

That evening each man received for the first and last time during the whole of the war, a full ration of beef, biscuit,tea, sugar and salt. Such luxuries none of us had indulged in for the past six weeks. From the commencement of the war up to this time, I believe we had lost more than one-third of our rations, and had been given positively to understand that we should have to pay the same amount every month whether we had any rations or not.This we found to be the case. At the end of every month, no matter whether we had received a half ration, quarter, and some days none whatever, the full amount was charged to the soldier.

June 2nd, '46. The Command of the Cavalry having been taken over by Major J. C. H. Gibson, 7th Dragoon Guards, the whole of the Cavalry was inspected by that Officer previous to marching out on patrol. Since the loss of the baggage train at Burns Hill each man had supplied himself with a small pot of some kind at his own expense for the purpose of boiling a little water for tea or coffee.The whole of the cooking utensils of the Division had been lost,and not one article had been replaced by the authorities. Each man carried his pot fastened to some part of his saddle most convenient to himself and as much out of the way as possible. Major Gibson, who had had as yet but little experience of bush fighting, objected to the men carrying those "abominable black pots" and ordered them to be taken off the saddles forthwith and made away with. Such an order in those days meant "instantly thrown away" or abide the consequence.

Several men murmured and ventured to appeal to a certain extent against this arbitrary order. I requested through the Captain of my Troop, to speak to the Major to whom I explained that those black pots were the only articles we had of any kind in which to cook our bit of food. The Government had not supplied us with any in place of

119

those lost with the baggage but I was abruptly cut short by the Major with these words:"Do as you are ordered sir, and make your complaint afterwards."—Any person with the slightest knowledge of what the Army was then will well understand its meaning.

Fortunately for us, there was an Officer near who on more than one occasion had been glad to get a drink of coffee from one of those "abominable black pots." This was Sir Harry Darrell of the 7th Dragoon Guards, as brave a soldier as ever drew a sword.

However by some means or other our grievance was communicated to the Officer Commanding the Division, Colonel Somerset, who sent for Major Gibson, and a few minutes after the order was given that we were at liberty to carry those "abominable black pots." The Dragoons and Cape Mounted Rifles were divided into two Divisions; one was ordered to Bok Kraal and the other to Trompetter's Bush. I went with the latter.

About mid-day we encountered a portion of Pato's Tribe, about 800. But the bush was too thick for the Cavalry to act with effect, although on such occasions we always dismounted and two-thirds of the men acted as Infantry, while the remainder took charge of the horses. The advance guard were driven in, and reported that a vast number of the enemy were advancing on the right and left fronts.

We were in a very bad position, the Kaffirs advancing on all sides of us, and there did not appear much chance of us getting out of it. But we were not aware or the arrangements made by that clever strategist in Kaffir warfare, Colonel Somerset. Just as our position had become most desperate, we heard the firing of Artillery and the rattle of musketry. This was the Artillery and Infantry from the Fort under the command of Colonel Somerset; and by a little skilful manoeuvring we managed to turn our position to excellent account.

The fighting did not last more than half an hour at close quarters, but we were some hours in pursuit of them. Several times they made a bit of a stand, but each time we drove them out of it.

As it was drawing near sunset, Colonel Somerset decided to remain where we were for the night, only retiring a short distance to where the bush was not so thick. We then began to make the best provision we could for the night, but all fires were to be out before darkness set in.

Major Gibson "had not the most remote idea" when he left the Fort that morning that he was going to pass the night in the bush. He was not prepared for it; had no provisions with him whatever. Now he had an opportunity to see the utility of those "abominable black pots" and I am perfectly satisfied,if one might judge by his appearance, that he would have been only too happy to have had a drink of warm coffee, even had it been made in one of the aforesaid "abominations."

June 3rd, '46. Were on the move again at daylight. Halted for about two hours at mid-day, then on again. But saw no Kaffirs and returned to the Fort at sunset.

The first English mail reached us since the war began. It had been brought up the country by reinforcements, mostly drafts from England."Susan" came to inform me that he had got a letter from his mother. Poor fellow, he was nearly beside himself with joy. His mother had sent him a box weighing nearly two hundred weight. One of the draft had brought it as far as Fort Beaufort, but there was no means of conveying it further. Among other things, it contained a medicine chest, a bottle of wine and a large plum cake. The news had such an effect on him that I don't believe he slept well for a month after.

June 7th. From the time we arrived at the Fort we had been employed day and night on patrol duty or conveying dispatches from one Camp to another from Fort Peddie to Fish River Mouth, Buffalo Mouth or Post Victoria.

The road to the latter was considered the most dangerous in all Kaffirland. The distance was about forty miles, sixteen miles of which was a thick bush. This was the most dangerous work we had. It was seldom that more than two men were sent with one dispatch,as it was generally believed that two men would ride through the bush with greater safety than six.The former would make less noise and not be so liable to excite suspicion, particularly in the bush. I was satisfied that if the Kaffirs made an attack two men would stand as good a chance as six.

With regard to health I had never enjoyed better in my life, but the heat of the sun punished me very much indeed. It took the skin completely off my face and more particularly my nose, and that is not so very prominent either. Most of us suffered in a similar manner.

Chapter Thirteen
Sword Point to Assegaie

This evening information was given by Umkoa— a Kaffir Chief who remained neutral throughout the whole of the war, though his Tribe did not—that it was the intention of the Chiefs Pato, Maccomo, Botman and Stock, with their Tribes estimated at 75,000 men, well armed with guns and assegaies, to attack a small Convoy of waggons which would pass through the Trompetter's Bush the following day.

On several occasions Umkoa had given valuable information to the Authorities. He never left the Fort himself; the information was brought to him by one of his Tribe who always appeared with a white cross on his forehead. He always had free ingress and egress to and from the Camp.

There was one thing which was rather singular. In all our beating about through the bush we never came across any of the Kaffir women and children, yet it was well known that the women used to supply the men with ammunition from their magazines.

June 8th, '46. Saddled up at 4 a.m. and, under the command of Colonel Somerset, marched towards the Kraal of Chief Stock, near the burial place of the great Chief Eno, for the purpose of drawing the attention of the Kaffirs from that part of the bush the convoy would pass through.

In that we were successful, as a large body of the enemy was observed only a short distance from us but as there was a very thick bush between us, it was thought advisable to reconnoitre a little before entering the bush. We tried several times to draw them out, but to no purpose.

The Artillery, up to this time kept out of sight, were now ordered to the front, and opened fire on the enemy with great effect. The Dragoons and Cape Mounted Rifles were ordered to dismount, and all that could be spared from guarding the horses entered the bush in skirmishing order and some desperate work ensued for about three hours, by which time we had driven them clean out of their favourite position.

We then returned as speedily as possible to our horses when suddenly another large body of the enemy was seen advancing on our right.

Sir Harry Darell wanted to give them battle, but Colonel Somerset would not sanction it as the enemy was too strong for such a small number of Dragoons—34. Some were of opinion that the number of Kaffirs in sight was 5,000, but I think 2,000 would be nearer the number. Our whole Force, consisted of Artillery two guns, 7th Dragoon Guards 34, Cape Mounted Rifles 98, Burghers 90, Fingoes 60, was now divided into two Divisions. The Artillery and Dragoons were not divided.

The whole Force advanced. Two Companies of the 91st Regiment which had been dispatched by another route from Fort Peddie now made their appearance on the heights. They had just arrived in the nick of time. The retreat of the Kaffirs was now completely cut off and they were nearly surrounded. No prisoners were wanted and very few escaped. By 1 p.m. not a Kaffir was to be seen.

We were then glad enough to hear that we were to retire a short distance from the bush, off-saddle our horses and refresh ourselves in the usual bush style—a lump of frizzled beef, a small piece of biscuit —our daily ration of which had been reduced to 8 ounces—a drink of warm and muddy water and, though the last, not the least of our comforts, a whiff of "The Fragrant Weed," that great consolation in the bush.

But we were doomed to disappointment. However hungry we might feel, there was something else to be done first. The Cape Mounted Rifles furnished the advance guard, the Artillery were in front covered by the Dragoons. A portion of the latter formed the Vedettes. The main body of the Cape Mounted Rifles was some little distance in the rear, as also the Burghers.

Suddenly the advance guard came in and reported that there was a large body of Kaffirs coming over the Gwanga flats right in front of us. Quite evidently they were coming to the assistance of those whom we had already routed. It was afterwards ascertained that it was the intention of this party to plunder the Convoy while the others were keeping, us employed. They were too late for that, but they were in time for us. The Dragoons having got somewhat clear of the bush, formed line and advanced.

On rising the ridge we caught sight of the Kaffirs, who could have had no idea of our approach. The number, according to the official report, was 800. Major Gibson was in command of the Cavalry, but I am under the impression that he was with the main body of the Cape Mounted Rifles as I have no recollection of seeing him after the middle of the day.

Sir Harry Darell gave the Trumpeter the order to sound "Trot," but this wild young Irish lad sounded the "Gallop." Sir Harry Darell and Lieut. P. M. Bunbury placed themselves in front of the Dragoons, and we advanced steadily. The Artillery were on the right flank. Who was in actual command of them at this time I cannot say. Two rounds of something was fired by them, when Captain Darell gave the word "Charge" and away we went.

The Kaffirs, finding escape hopeless and shouting *Mah Wo*," formed themselves into a compact body and steadily waited our approach. We opened out as much as possible in order to prevent them catching us in a trap.

The Kaffirs allowed us to get within about thirty yards, when they fired a volley. The shots went whistling over our heads like a flight of birds. Had they known anything of their weapons and at that distance have used the assegaie instead of the old flint guns, not a single man could have escaped. As it was, we had 7 men and 11 horses wounded.

We dashed in among them. It was now the sword against the assegaie. We cut our way clean through them. Captain Walpole, Royal Engineers, bravely drew his sword and joined us in the charge Captain Darell, Captain Walpole and Lt. P. M. Bunbury were all wounded in the first charge.

About this time the Cape Mounted Rifles and Burghers came up, but the former could not charge the enemy, as they had no swords. These were lost with the baggage at Burns Hill; they had been taken from the Totties as they were to them a useless appendage, and placed in the waggons.

From the 8th of June, 1846, to 1882, which is thirty-six years, this assertion of mine was never contradicted, although many letters which I have written in reference to that war were published in the *Naval and Military Gazette* during the years 1853 to 1856. But within the last two years I have been informed that I am in error regarding the Cape Mounted Rifles; that they "did join in the charge on the Gwanga Flats on the 8th June, 1846." I still maintain that they did not.

Like the justly celebrated Balaclava Charge, with all the deaths that have taken place among the survivors of that terrible day during the number of years that have elapsed, if all who claim the honour of participating in the charge could be brought together this day, I have no doubt we should still have more than the actual number engaged. I must ask pardon for this digression, but I felt it was necessary. I will certainly admit that the Cape Mounted Rifles did considerable execution with their double-barrelled carbines; and the Burghers, I believe, did not waste a single round of their ammunition.

In charging through the Kaffirs the second time, I got a very ugly assegaie through my left leg just above the knee joint which penetrated the saddle panels and entered between the ribs of my beautiful horse, Spider. Some man passing struck the shaft of the assegaie with his sword, thinking to knock it out, but it held too fast in the saddle.

Spider appeared anything but comfortable with the assegaie sticking so close to his ribs, and it took me all my time to keep my seat. At length a man seized hold of the shaft and drew it out, but unfortunately not the same way it went in. He had turned it round just enough to make a cross cut of it, and the jagged edges of the blade made a very ugly wound.

The whole force now pursued the Kaffirs, who fled in all directions; and the plain being very large, there could not have been many who succeeded in reaching the bush. It was almost worthwhile being placed *hors de combat* to view the scene which presented itself. I caught sight of Lieut. Bunbury and rode toward him. He appeared badly wounded. He gave me some brandy from his flask and, telling me I had better "make for the rear," galloped off— I believe in search of the Trumpeter, who had bolted and joined the Burghers in the chase.

"Make for the rear," I thought to myself; yes, but where is the rear? That was the puzzler. At length, being in considerable pain and somewhat weak from loss of blood, I began to look about me for the best road out of the way. But turn which way I would, the Kaffirs were in front of me. At length I made for one point where I thought I had the best chance, when suddenly a Kaffir rose from the ground and threw an assegaie which entered the shoulder of poor Spider.

I managed to pull it out,then rode to the place where the Kaffir lay flat on his back. Thinking he might be acting, I drove my sword through his body; but, sure enough, he was dead.The last act of his life had been for revenge.

I rode about the plain for some time. I knew not which direction to take and at last I came to a stand I had not tasted food or water that day. At length I was picked up by the Trumpeter and two Dutch Burghers who had been sent in search of me. I believe Lt. Bunbury had given the information where I had last been seen.

By the time I reached the main body, all the wounded had been sent to the hospital at Fort Peddie. I was placed on the limbers of one of the guns, and I remembered no more until I found myself in the hospital hut at Fort Peddie.

Chapter Fourteen
The Best Shot in the Regiment

The place was full of wounded Dragoons, Cape Mounted Rifles and Dutch Burghers. The latter had joined the Army as Volunteers. The stench of the place was terrible. There were little or no medical stores. Some old sheeting was sent by the Station Commissioner, Captain Maclean, to be torn up for bandages. The Missionary of the Station was unremitting in his attention to the wounded. I regret that I cannot speak positively as to his name, because he was so exceedingly kind to all of us. Day and night, he was nearly always present.

The provisions which we had brought to the Fort had nearly all been sent on to the different Camps, and now we were as bad off as ever. Operations and amputations were going on daily. One morning I fully expected that my turn had come. The two Surgeons were standing beside me in consultation. Fortunately for me they could not agree. The younger, Doctor Monroe, was for amputation; the elder, Doctor Hathaway, was of a different opinion and from that day I was entirely under his charge. I can safely say this: during the whole time of my service I never knew two Medical Officers that were as skilful, kind and attentive to the patients under their charge as Surgeon Hathaway and Assistant Surgeon Monroe of the 91st Regiment.

My old friend "Susan" was among the wounded. He had been stabbed by a Kaffir with an assegaie in his bridle hand, which was lacerated very much. But I believe "Susan" paid for this kindly attention by putting his sword through the Kaffir's body.

For some days the wound in my leg continued very bad. Several times I believe the Surgeon had his doubts about curing it. I got plenty of cauterizing, two and three times a day. The Surgeon often said: "You may thank God you have a constitution that would bear twice as much."

Once when I was grumbling at the cool manner in which he was rubbing the caustic backward and forward through the hole in my leg he said:

"If I hear any more of your grumbling I will take the leg off altogether, and then there will be an end of it."

After that I was obliged to be careful what I said.

July 3rd, '46. A report reached the Fort (Peddie) through the Chief before mentioned (Umkoa) that it was the intention of the Kaffirs to attack the Fort, more particularly the Star Fort. where there was a considerable quantity of ammunition stored.

All the worst cases among the wounded were ordered removed into this Fort for safety. There was only three left in the hospital hut, namely myself, a blind man and a Dutch Burgher who had lost one arm. The order given by the Surgeon was to be carried out as follows for our safety:

As soon as the alarm was given the blind man was to take me upon his back, and the man with one arm was to lead him into the Fort, a distance of about 50 yards.

About midnight the alarm was given, and away we went as per order received. We had scarcely time to get inside the Fort when the Kaffirs came down and made the attack, the sole object of which was to get possession of the ammunition.

But they did not succeed. In the deep trench which surrounded the Fort there was concealed three Companies of the 91st Regiment waiting to receive them, and they met with a very warm reception. The Kaffirs were driven back, but only for a time as within half an hour they rushed down again and into the trench, and again they were driven out. They did not come back the third time.

98 dead bodies were found the following morning and buried by the Fingoes in a *kloof* a short distance from the

Fort, but they had dragged away all the wounded they could get a hold of during the night.

July 7th, '46. "Susan" came to bid me good-bye. He had recovered and was proceeding to join a Division at Fish River Mouth.

During the time I was in the Hospital the Officers in the Fort were very kind to me, lending me books to read, etc., more particularly Sir Harry Darell and Lieut. Bunbury, 7th Dragoon Guards, Captain Bringhirst, 45th Regiment, and Lieut. King, Royal Artillery.

One day I asked the Surgeon, Dr. Hathaway— whose kindness and attention I shall ever remember— if he would try and get me a crutch and stick as I was anxious to make a move toward getting out of the Hospital. The Surgeon said he did not know how he could manage that, but at all events he would see about it.

I also asked Sir Harry Darell, who said:

"I'll see what I can do. If my arm is strong enough I will make you a crutch, if I can only get the tools."

The following day Sir Harry brought me a crutch, and shortly afterwards a stick, and I began to get about a little. And the Surgeon was kind enough to let me leave the Hospital and take up my quarters in the Dragoons' Barracks, which was a considerable distance from the Hospital, and also he visited me every day.

One day Sir Harry informed me that, as the Officers had received supplies from Graham's Town, it was their intention of dining together the following evening, and asked me if I would come and sing for their amusement. Of course I was able to sing, but was not able to walk the distance, even with the aid of my crutch.

However, I set to work and made out my programme, among which were two new songs I had composed while in the Hospital— *"The Battle of the Gwanga,"* and *"A Soldier's Life in the Bush."*

The evening came and I was taken to the Officers'

marquee in a barrow and was seated in an easy chair close under the wall of their tent. My songs were invariably well received. Each of my new compositions gained an encore and sundry glasses of wine. At the conclusion I was called into the Officers' tent, but as I had not brought my crutch I was unable to comply with the call. But the chair I was sitting upon had castors on the feet, and I was wheeled into the presence of the Officers. I was highly complimented for my singing, especially my new compositions, and was requested by several of the Officers to furnish them with copies; to which I consented providing they would supply me with the paper needful. A quantity of silver from a tray which was on the table was then handed to me, after which I was at liberty to go to my quarters.

When we started I noticed that the man who was wheeling my barrow was twisting it about in a very peculiar manner. Several times I spoke to him, but could get no answer. Twice he stopped and drank from a bottle he carried inside the breast of his jacket. I questioned him:

"Where did you get that bottle from?"

He replied: "Mind your own business."

When we reached the middle of the plain between the Officers' Mess and the Barracks he tumbled me out of the barrow on the ground and, quietly seating himself in the barrow, prepared to compose himself for sleep. I then found out that by some means he had possessed himself of a bottle of brandy, part of which he had drank together with the wine which had been sent to me, which l did not drink as the Surgeon told me not to take more than one glass, neither did I.

It was useless to try to persuade him to take me home. He appeared to have made up his mind to stop there, and there was no alternative but I must stop also until he chose to move, as my leg was so bad I could not bear the weight of my body on it. Several times I tried to rouse him and at length succeeded, when he jumped up in a passion and walked off with the barrow, leaving me sitting on the ground. I thought to myself, here is a chance for a stray Kaffir. I could tell by the sound of the wheel that he did not go far before he again stopped. Here he appeared to have made up his mind to have his sleep out without further annoyance. I shouted to him repeatedly but received no answer until daybreak, when he brought back the barrow and made all sorts of apologies for his conduct.

But when we reached the Barracks the Corporal in charge of the guard made him a prisoner, and at mid-day he was taken before Sir Harry Darell and I was obliged to state the whole affair. The man would have been severely punished only I put as good a face on the matter as possible and he got off with a moderate light punishment.

When I counted the money I found I had received £5.12. Out of this I gave the man with the barrow 5 shillings, and also gave 30 shillings to be divided among the men who had attended me the first month I was in the Hospital.

During the following month I made a considerable sum by my doggerel composition,and saved £17.I had also spent a great deal, as about this time a Trader had arrived at the Port with three waggons laden with stores. He had "run the gauntlett"from Graham's Town and I decided to indulge in a few luxuries such as I had not tasted for some months past. Such another opportunity might not occur for a very long time of getting such things at any price. Accordingly I purchased 50 Ibs. of flour at 1s.2d. per lb.,5 lbs., of raisins at 1s. 1d. per lb., 4 lbs. of sugar at 1s. 2d. per lb., 6 lbs. of common biscuits at 1s. 4d. per lb., 1 lb. of tea 8s., and one dozen bottles of porter at 2s. 8d.per bottle, in all £5.17.The last two articles were utterly useless.The tea stank, and the porter was like vinegar.

The Kaffirs continued to be exceedingly attentive to us. They did not let us have one night in peace. Although their shots done no harm, they annoyed us very much and prevented us from getting any rest. Many times, had they only known it, they might have got into the Dragoons' Barracks and cleared every thing out of it, when the only occupants had been myself and two or three other cripples, all the remainder of the men being out patrolling or on dispatch or express duty. At such times we cripples were posted on the walls, each furnished with a box of grenades, in addition to our arms, and plenty of ammunition.

One night I saw a Kaffir driving a bullock. He was a considerable distance from me. Now and then the moon shone very bright. I did not like the idea of losing such a chance, at the same time there was one round of ammunition to account for. While I was thus thinking the Kaffir was getting farther away, and presently I lost sight of him altogether. He was then crossing the drift near the house of the Missionary. I waited until he made his appearance on the rising ground at the other side, then, resting the barrel of my gun on the wall, I took aim and fired.

The Kaffir disappeared and the bullock deliberately walked away. But as the moon was somewhat over clouded just then the Kaffir was not discernible. But when the Patrol was coming in next morning they came across the Kaffir. He was dead. I had shot him through the centre of the back. When this affair was reported to the Officer Commanding I was highly complimented for my vigilence and for the excellent shot I had made. The "best shot in the Regiment," a Troop Sergeant Major called Moffat praised me also. His right arm had recently been amputated. He had not long been married. The history of Mrs. Moffat was somewhat romantic.

She was the daughter of a fisherman, and from her childhood had been much attached to a youth about her own age. His name was John Marvell. He suddenly disappeared from the village. Ann—Mrs. Moffat—was always under the impression that he had gone to sea. One day she also disappeared.

A vessel with Troops was on the voyage from England to the Cape of Good Hope when a youth who had been employed in the cabin fell from the foreyard onto the deck, and was taken below, when the discovery was made that it was a female.

A lady on board, wife of an Officer of the 91st Regiment, took a great liking to Ann and took her as servant; and on their arrival in the Colony, Ann accompanied her Mistress to Fort Beaufort, where the 2nd Battalion of the 91st were stationed. Ann had been some time in her situation and was a great favourite with her Master and Mistress, and to them she had related her history—how she had run away from home with her brother's clothes and had been two sea voyages as assistant to the steward.

One day she returned to the house with the children when her Mistress noticed that she was very pale and questioned as to the cause. But it was a considerable time before she could obtain a satisfactory answer. At length she asked her Mistress if she knew the name of the man who was on sentry on her Master's quarters.

As a matter of course the lady did not, but when her Master returned he procured the names of all the men who had been on sentry at his quarters during that day. But the name that Ann expected to find was not among them. At length the Officer questioned one of the men very closely as to his name, when the man acknowledged that he had enlisted under an assumed name and that his right name was John Marvell.

He was a man of good character and a smart soldier and was accordingly promoted. Much to his surprise he was introduced to his old sweetheart; and it was agreed that when he attained the rank of Sergeant in due course he was to have leave to get married.

All things went on very pleasantly until the day before the wedding was to have taken place. When John was returning to the Station for the purpose, he had to cross a river, and in doing so was carried away by the flood and drowned. And Ann eventually became the wife of Troop Sergeant Major Samuel Moffat, 7th Dragoon Guards.

Chapter Fifteen
I Come Close to Death

October 11th, 1846. My leg having got pretty strong again and the duty being very hard on the few Dragoons that were stationed in Fort Peddie, I made up my mind to try and do a little and informed the Surgeon of my intention. The Doctor said he thought a short journey would not do me any harm, but that I was not fit for a longer one.

However, that evening an express came in that was to be forwarded to the General at Victoria Post instanter. The distance was 47 miles. There was only three men—Dragoons—on the Post beside me; the remainder were on patrol or express duty. Was I strong enough to go the journey, 47 miles as fast as the horses could go? That was the question I was to answer, which I did by deciding to make the attempt, and three of us started at 9 p.m. We had not got more than 12 miles when my leg became very painful, which increased to the most excruciating agony. In passing through the 16 mile bush at *Foona's Kloof* several shots were fired at us, but the darkness favoured us, and only one shot took effect, slightly grazing the hindquarters of one of the horses. We reached the Post at 4 a.m. I was lifted from my horse and placed under the waggon, where I remained some time, until I was seen by some men of the 27th Regiment, who immediately carried me to their tent—and I may here remark that I never knew before or since such good feeling to exist between a Cavalry and Infantry Regiment as there was between the 7th Dragoon Guards and the 27th Regiment.

I remained in the tent until evening, when we were ordered to saddle up at once and return to Fort Peddie with a return dispatch. I was obliged to be lifted on to my horse. Our orders were to go as fast as the horses were able.

The agony I endured that night,I shall never forget.Twice I fell off my horse. Both wounds had burst and I was bleeding freely—and that nasty 16 miles of thick bush to go through. I was well satisfied that, happen what might, my companions would not leave me behind while life or chance remained.

Before entering the bush they dismounted, and with the whole of the baggage straps from the saddles they fastened me to the saddle as securely as possible. One of them rode on each side of me and held me by the arm. I have not the slightest recollection of reaching Fort Peddie, but a few days afterwards memory returned and I found myself again in the Hospital hut and my head had been shaved. I was informed by Doctor Hathaway that I had had a very narrow escape.

Nov. 6th, '46. I was ordered to be removed to Cawoods Post, four days' journey in a waggon drawn by 12 oxen. One English horse would draw as much as 12 bullocks, but the horse would starve while the oxen would fatten.

I got along remarkably well on the road.There were only three of us—me, the Hottentot driver and the little forelooper.There was only one gun and about 140 rounds of ammunition between the three of us. Had the Kaffirs have come upon us we should have been a very easy prey.While on the road I shot a few ducks and peafowl,so we fared most sumptuously. I was the provider, the driver was the cook, the little forelooper was the coolie to fetch water and break up wood for the fire.

In due course I arrived at my destination. There was a small detachment of Dragoons and Cape Mounted Rifles stationed there for the purpose of keeping open the road between Graham's Town and Kaffirland via Fish River Mouth.

Among the Dragoons were a few men of the draft which had recently arrived from the depot at Maidstone, and I was quite proud to be able to say that I was the shortest and lightest man in the Regiment no longer.Two of them were the smallest specimens of Heavy Dragoons I had yet seen. But that generous act of the "Iron Duke"—demon, I might have said—which fixed the term of service of the Cavalry man at 28 years for a pension of sixpence per day, had brought the animated food for powder to such a miserable state in the market that the authorities were actually glad to get anything that would answer the purpose of "ball-stoppers."

The Kaffirs frequently visited us at night, and invariably one or two were found dead the following morning. I very soon began to gather strength again, and passed a great deal of my time in the bush surrounding the old farm house.

Vegetation about that part of the country was truly beautiful. It abounded in game—springbok, wild duck and peafowl. On these little excursions I was invariably accompanied by three or four Hottentots, and, being a pretty good hand with a gun, I was never in want of powder and shot. The Totties kept me well supplied for which I furnished game. They were always pleased and most willing to assist me at all times. There was a cause for this kindness which I cannot now explain, but the name of *Kychee* was sufficient at all times to get anything done that I might want.

Many hours have I passed listening to the wild tales of these extraordinary people. At this time I was able to converse with them in their own language quite fluently. They are a race of people with little or no pretension to beauty, their females in particular, with their huge posterior, thick lips, high cheek bones and very low foreheads. They have the name of being the most depraved of the African races, but, however depraved they may be, I know there are exceptions even among them.

Within half a mile of the old house we occupied, there was an African hotel kept by a Dutchman whose name was Tims. He had a large family of grown-up sons and daughters, with whom I have spent some very pleasant days. The moment I made my appearance in front of the house one of the family would come out to assist me up the steps. I always spent Sunday with them. We had Divine Service morning and evening. All the family could sing. One of the sons played the flute.

I obtained leave to spend a fortnight with them; and during my stay one of the daughters was married to a Dutchman who had come all the way from Colesberg to marry her. The parting from her parents, brothers and sisters was very affecting. The bride was 27 years of age, and if I was asked to judge her weight, I should say about 16 stone. Her husband also was very stout. They certainly were not the most delicate couple I ever saw. I had not spent more than half of the time for which I had obtained leave when I was obliged to return to the Post. My leg had begun to gather again. I had to be carried on a litter and one night very shortly after both wounds burst, and there is no doubt I should have bled to death had it not been for a man who was laying near me at the time and made the discovery. After this I was ordered to be sent in to Fort Beaufort Hospital.

A covered waggon and oxen was procured, and as there was another man who was very bad with dysentery and there being no Medical Officer with the Detachment, we were to be sent in together. A few pounds of meat and some biscuit were put into the waggon as provisions for the road. We were four days on the journey, the horrors of which make me shudder when I think of them. We were both utterly helpless, and not a soul with us—only the Hottentot driver and his forelooper. We were entirely covered with maggots, and nearly worried to death by the thousands of flies attracted by the horrible stench of the waggon. When we reached the Hospital we were carried into the Dead House, stripped and washed. My companion died, I believe, the following day. I was placed under a Surgeon—Dr. Fouker—who had but very recently arrived from England, and I went under another course of cutting and burning.

With cleanliness and medical attention I soon began to recover again, but as my case was considered very doubtful my name was put on the list of men "To be Discharged from the Service," but as I recovered beyond all expectation, my name was withdrawn. It was not my wish to be discharged as I liked the Service very well.

December 21st, 1846. Having got pretty strong again, I was sent to join a Division at Fort Hare under Sir Peregrine Maitland.

Dec. 22nd. The Division marched from Fort Hare, our destination being the Kei River—commonly called by the Troops Starvation River—to punish the Kaffir Chief Kreli, who was known to have in his territory the whole of the cattle belonging to the Tribes with which we were at war, having been sent there for safekeeping.

Dec. 25th. It was nearly sunset before we came to any water. There were no oxen to disturb it, still it was like so much mud. The horses were let loose for grazing, and the same might have been done with the men for all we had got to eat. Having come a great distance during the day, the waggons containing the provisions had not come up, therefore we had to content ourselves with another "hot supper"— a smoke of the pipe, a drink of muddy water, and squat under a bush for the night. Christmas Day and not a morsel of food to eat! I was still in the same Division with "Susan," and I was sitting under a bush smoking my pipe when he came to me. As a matter of course he was very hungry, and as usual began the old story—how many plum puddings and mince pies would be made at home, and how many there would be to partake of them.

"Ah," said he, "I remember one Christmas when Pa served me with part of the leg of a goose. It was a joint I never liked, and I told Pa so, when I was ordered to leave the table. Don't I wish I had the leg of a goose now."

By what I knew of "Susan's" appetite, I should think two legs of a goose would have stood a very poor chance with him at that moment. I should not have felt disposed to have given much for what he would leave of them. He had made several attempts to learn to smoke tobacco, but each time it had made him ill. I endeavoured to persuade him to have another try, particularly as it was Christmas Day. I did not wish to see him ill, but anything was preferable to being annoyed about goose legs when one has nothing to eat and feels particularly hungry.

The waggons reached us at midnight and at day light the rations were issued, viz 11/2 lbs. meat and 8 oz. of biscuit, which quantity had been our daily allowance since we left Fort Hare.

Dec. 31st, '46. At the Seaside near the mouth of the Kei River. Here four days. Biscuit was served out to each man at the rate of 6 oz.per day and at the same time it was intimated to us that it was not at all improbable but that we should have to make it last for a longer period than four days,as we were going somewhere, but none knew where. The whole of our Camp Equipage was to be left behind under a Guard,and we were to trust to the elements, each man taking as much ammunition as he could carry. At last it came out that we were going to enter Kreli's country as soon as it was dark.

But at that time the rain came down very fast and we were obliged to stand and hold our horses until near daylight, when it began somewhat to abate and we made a start for the River, which was about two miles distant through the thickest bush I ever saw.

When we reached the River we found it so much swollen by the recent heavy rain that it was not possible that we could get across with our Artillery and we dare not return to show ourselves crossing the open ground between the bush and our Camp. Consequently there was no alternative but to remain concealed in the bush until the River should fall sufficiently to enable us to get across.

January 1st, 1847. Delightful prospect for the New Year— the strength and efficiency of Heavy Dragoons to be maintained on 6 ounces of biscuit per day!

The water in the River having fallen, we succeeded in getting across—all except one man, the rough riding

Sergeant, Andrew Ritchie, whose horse when in the centre of the River became restive and they were both carried away by the current and lost. He was a married man. His wife was the daughter of the Quarter-Master of the Regiment; and she subsequently became the wife of another Sergeant of the Regiment, the present Private Secretary to the Duke of Westminster. His name is Colonel David Scotland. It was near sunset when the whole had crossed the River. We then marched about 4 miles into Kreli's country and halted for the night. The horses were placed in lines, 12 in each. They were fastened to each other by their head collars, one man to each flank horse, and one man in front and one in rear of the centre of the line. The latter two men were to keep the horses from moving forward or backward. After revelling in the usual bush luxuries of frizzled beef and muddy water, we coiled up under a bush and consoled ourselves with a whiff of the Fragrant Weed. During the night we were reinforced by a party of Hottentots under the command of Captain Hogg, 7th Dragoon Guards, also a number of Burghers under the command of Sir Andreas Stockenstrom.

January 2nd, 1847. Moved on again at daylight, but very slowly in consequence of the bush being so very thick and the rain, which fell heavily. At length we were obliged to halt. The ground was so bad that we could not get along and the bush so very thick. The Infantry got in the shelter of the bush as much as possible, and the Cavalry stood holding their horses. We remained in this not very comfortable position eleven hours.

January 3rd. Moved on again at 3 a.m. towards the Seaside. At 11 a.m. we caught sight of a vast number of cattle grazing on the hills at some distance from us. 30 Dragoons and 50 Cape Mounted Rifles were sent off in pursuit; a number of Infantry were sent off in another direction. It was the roughest ground I ever rode over, full of rocks and gullies. We were some time in reaching the cattle. There were not more than 50 Kaffirs guarding them and as soon as they caught sight of us they raised the cry *"Rooi Badjies"*—Red Coats—and away they went as fast as their legs would carry them. None of them were armed. Thus it was evident we were not expected. We surrounded the cattle and began driving them towards the Division, which was very far from being an easy job. The Hottentots are first-rate hands at driving cattle.

The alarm was soon given by the Kaffirs. We could see them gathering on all sides, and making their way towards a ravine through which we should be obliged to pass. But fortunately the Infantry was there, and when the Kaffirs reached it they met with a very disagreeable surprise. We succeeded in getting the whole of the cattle through. Three of the Infantry were wounded, one very badly. When we joined the main body we found we had got about 1,100 of the finest cattle I ever saw. These were handed over to the Hottentot Levy to be escorted back to the Colony.

January 4th, 1847. Moved on again at daylight. Still raining fast, which made it anything but pleasant marching through a thick bush. It was bad enough for the Cavalry but it was tenfold worse for the Infantry as many of them were getting bad off for shoe leather.

This day we saw neither Kaffirs nor cattle, and at night we crouched down under a bush, our clothes all in rags, and wet to the skin. We had been five days subsisting on one pound, eight ounces of biscuit. We were all free from gout—that was one good thing.

The Troops had liberty to slaughter what cattle they chose. All hands were living entirely on beef, which is not the most palatable food one could wish, without salt or a particle of vegetable of any kind. I can assert as a positive fact that on that Campaign many times I have known cattle to be alive, slaughtered, frizzled and eaten within one hour. More than once I have eaten meat raw with the hot blood running from it. The hard living, together with exposure, caused several deaths from dysentery.

143

January 5th. We reached a deserted Missionary Station—Butterworth—and were much pleased to find six waggons laden with provisions which had been brought up country by an escort of the Rifle Brigade. These were the kind of soldiers for Kaffir warfare. They were the very terror of all Kaffirs, who dreaded the sight of a *Zwart Badjie*—Black Jacket. Still, a Kaffir war could not be carried on without Cavalry and Artillery.

This day each man received $2^1/_4$ lbs. of biscuit. This was to be considered as a six-days ration. Some of the men were simple enough to ask for the 6 ozs for the 4th inst. as they had not received any for that day. But they got the same answer they had often had before, namely, "No back rations allowed." But if there was "no back rations were allowed," when the end of the month came the full amount for the full ration of the soldier was charged to him—30 or 31 days'—according to the number in the month—rations at so much per day—and no question as to what was allowed was answered or entertained.

I do not mean to say that a man was not allowed to ask a question, but I mean it was not advisable for a man to be too inquisitive in the Army. He would not find it conducive to his comfort and it was also necessary that he should swallow a pill occasionally that was extremely nauseous to a man with the very slightest knowledge of one of the very simplest rules in arithmetic. Not quite so bad as the Totty with his felt scoons, "one pair for this foot and one pair for that;" but if a man was told that 2 and 2 1/2 added made, it would be as well for his future comfort not to argue the point too closely or it might very probably affect him through the whole of his career in the Service by getting him the name of being a "lawyer." He might be recommended for promotion a hundred times, but to no purpose. "He will never do, Sir, he's a lawyer;" and once in possession of that title he was seldom clear of prison or punishment of some kind. Still, I knew a man who once bore that title for many years who had the respect of nearly every Officer in his Regiment, and was nearly 24 years in the Service without ever once being a defaulter, but I expect his style of law must have been somewhat different to that in common. However, they kept him nearly 12 years a Private before he got any promotion.

January 6th and 7th, 1847. Two days we were obliged to remain stationary. The weather was so very bad it was impossible to get through the bush. I cannot imagine the Army was in such a wretched state during the Peninsular War, as we were at this time—our clothes torn to rags, exposed to the heavy rains day and night, and to subsist on six ounces of biscuit per day with any quantity of meat but not a vessel of any kind to cook or boil it in. No tea, coffee or vegetables of any kind. Several of the Infantry were without shoes. The general appearance of the whole, both Cavalry and Infantry, was wretched in the extreme,

This day Sir Peregrine Maitland left us for England, heartily tired of bush fighting.

Jan. 8th, 1847. Marched in the direction of the Kraal of the Chief, Kreli. About midday we caught sight of a number of cattle only a short distance off, which were captured with little trouble. The number was about 1,600 and in splendid condition. They had been grazing for the past eight months on what was considered the finest pasturage in all Kaffirland. They belonged to the Paramount Chief of the Gaika Tribes, Sandilla, and had been sent there for safety, where they would most probably have remained had it not been for the information given by the neutral Chief Umkoa.

Chapter Sixteen
War Against Kreli's Kaffirs

War was now declared against Kreli. His Tribe was very strong. He boasted that he could bring 30,000 men into the field, all well armed, and it was well known that they were a superior race to the Gaika Tribes.

Jan. 9th. The spoor—track—of more cattle having been discovered, we followed it and found that it led to a dense bush. The infantry advanced direct to their front. The Cavalry dismounted, one man leading three horses, the remainder following the spoor to the right and the Dutch Burghers to the left front.

Very shortly we heard the Infantry firing, and directly afterwards a few shots from the Burghers. Then we caught sight of a few Kaffirs, but could not get near them. At length we made the discovery that these fellows were only diverting us, while another body of the enemy were driving a great drove of cattle in another direction.

The Dragoons and Burghers mounted their horses and gave chase. The Infantry made a short cut through the ravine. After about one hour's good fighting the Kaffirs made a clean run for it, and we came to the conclusion that Kreli's men were not to be compared with the Gaikas for close work.

We got about 1,700 very fine cattle. The Kreli's managed to carry off nearly the whole of their wounded, but they left nearly 200 dead on the field.

When we halted for the night, sleep was out of the question. We had not been allowed to make any fires, consequently had not the trouble of cooking any food or the trouble of eating any. The Kaffirs kept up a continuous fire the whole night, not ceasing until some time after daylight the following day. Three of our horses and several of the cattle were wounded. I made two or three very good shots that day.

I may here remark that the Kaffirs at this time had but very little knowledge of the use of firearms. Very few of them fired their gun from the shoulder but discharged it from the hip, with the muzzle elevated so much that their shots nearly all went over our heads. They had not the most remote idea what quantity of powder was necessary for one charge. They would empty the powder from a bullock's horn into the palm of the hand and pour it into the barrel. They were equally ignorant in reference to shot. Anything that could be got into the barrel was satisfactory to them. It was evident that, however well they might be off for powder, they were very short of ball, particularly lead. A great portion of their shot was made of zinc, with the casting nipple uncut, or chain links cut in pieces of various lengths.

One day a dog that had followed me for some days was killed close beside me. The wound had such a peculiar appearance and was so large that I opened the body to see what had caused it, when I found he had been killed by the bowl of an iron spoon which had been rolled up small enough to be put into the gun barrel. Nearly the whole of the guns taken from the Kaffirs at different times had the Tower Mark upon them and all other marks the same as the old Brown Bess. I often thought it somewhat strange that no one ever made themselves sufficiently inquisitive as to enquire by what means these guns came into possession of the Kaffirs.

January, 10th, '47. Our force was divided into two Divisions, the first to act as advance guard and for reconnoitering, and the second for the immediate charge of the cattle.

About midday we unexpectedly came to the skirts of the bush and saw a number of cattle grazing on a plain beyond, distant about half a mile, and a thick bush on the far side of them. I never felt the sun so hot as it was on this day. The bush was like a furnace. Not a Kaffir was to be seen. What had become of them? We were perfectly satisfied they had never left that number of cattle grazing without some guard over them. The order was sent back to bring up half of the Second Division, and the remainder to halt with the cattle for further orders. The Cape Mounted Rifles and the Dutch Burghers were ordered to advance from both flanks the bush extending some distance in each direction. The preconcerted signal having been given, the Dragoons darted out and across the plain at a gallop.

I never saw such a sight. The bush was swarming with Kaffirs. Had they been any sort of marksmen at all, not one of us would have got away from them. The firing was begun by the Cape Mounted Rifles and Burghers, which set the cattle rushing in all directions The Kaffirs fought as they never did before. They seized hold of the reins of our horses and did not release them until their skull was cleft in two or the sword driven through their body. Twice they all but succeeded in getting the cattle from us into the bush. A Kaffir seized hold of my bridle and I drove my sword through his body. He caught hold of the blade at his breast and held it fast for some few seconds before he fell from the blade, dead.

At length we succeeded in getting possession of the cattle, about 800 and drove to the rear.

It was now quite evident that it would take us all our time to guard the prize we had. We now began to countermarch toward the Kei River with nearly 800 of the best cattle in the country.

Our horses by this time, through hard work and exposure and very little food, began to drop on the road, when they were immediately shot to prevent them falling into the hands of the enemy. The saddles and bridles were removed and fastened on the backs of the Kaffirs' riding bullocks, which were always known from the rest by having a rhiem fastened round their girth which the Kaffir holds to prevent the bullock from throwing him off. About midnight we halted, and directly after the Kaffirs began firing the same as on the previous night. We dare not make a fire to frizzle a piece of beef, therefore were obliged once more to fall back on the "hot supper."

At daybreak I saw some of the Riflemen going from bush to bush. They were eating something, that was quite evident. Whatever could it be that had turned up? Such a slice of luck! I found it was the gum from the mimosa tree they were eating. I did not take any myself as I did not retain a very pleasing recollection of the first and only time I dined off that "luxury" which gave me the jaws ache for a week afterwards.

At daylight we were allowed to make fires. Some bullocks were shot, and they were very soon cut up and frizzling on the fire. Out of our whole Force, I don't believe there was one man that had tasted a biscuit for the past three days. I know I had not.

Jan. 11th, '47. In order to give the men a little time to cook some meat, we did not move before 11 a.m., and then the rain came down like a flood. Still we pushed on as well as could be expected considering the number of cattle with which we were encumbered and the continued annoyance from the Kaffirs, who never ceased firing at us. Had but one half of their shots taken effect, we should have been cleared off long ago.

At night we halted, but no fires were allowed. We did not want them as most of us had provided a little extra in the morning. At midnight we moved on again, in order to get out of Kreli's country to the place where we had left our waggons on the 31st of December.

We reached them at daylight and found they contained a small quantity of biscuit, which was ordered to be issued at the rate of four ounces to each man; but although it was most carefully weighed, even to the shaking of the bags, many had to go without.

January 12th, 1847. Fires were made. Some of the best bullocks were shot,cut up and distributed among us and as I had been so fortunate as to get the four ounces of biscuit, I revelled in these luxuries to my heart's content.

But the rain came down very heavily, yet, thank God rain never hurt me. Many a poor fellow could not say as much.It was quite impossible we could move until the rain had somewhat abated.

Two men were reported as having died during the past night from dysentery. Did they die last night or did they drop on the road and were left to die and only missed this morning? Exposure and starvation was doing its worst among the Troops. Great God, the appearance of many was horrible to look at! Death was plainly visible in the faces of some, and starvation and disease in many. The Medical Officers could do nothing.They had no medicine.There was no conveyance for the sick and wounded. Our only way of conveying such cases was by fastening them on the back of a horse. In short, sick and wounded men were not considered worth the trouble they gave in those days. Several horses had died of starvation within the last 48 hours.

The past three days we had been expecting provisions would have reached us from Block Drift, but they had not arrived.About 11 a.m., the rain having somewhat abated, we made another move and staggered on until 4 p.m., at which time we reached The Springs so named on account of the number of springs about there.

I cannot say that we particularly stood in need of water, having been wet to the skin for the last three days. Such a wretched lot of human being as soldiers I should think was never seen before or since. One half of the Infantry were without boots, but most of them had adopted a very novel substitute by fastening two pieces of green hide together the length of the foot or rather more.This is done with a strip of the same. Some of the men made them with three pieces of hide, two for the sole and one for the upper, having,with the aid of a knife, roughly stitched the pieces together all round the edges, a hole being made at one end of the top piece, the foot is inserted. Being soft it sat close to the shape of the foot, and in a few hours would set as hard as possible. Of course they had to be tied securely to the foot and they were not easily removed when once they had got set. With regard to the Dragoons, such a lot of scarecrows was never seen. Nearly two-thirds of them were on foot with the Infantry, their horses having been shot on the road.

This evening we had something to cheer us. Two waggons laden with meal, tea and sugar had arrived; and each man received 8 ozs. of meal, 1/2 oz of tea and 4 ozs. of sugar. Whoever could have been the author of such extravagance I could not imagine as to send us such luxuries as these. As Paddy said, "More power to 'em, say Oi." We had permission to have fires as long as the Kaffirs thought proper to allow us, which was about 10 p.m., then they made up for lost time. They began with a few straggling shots, which they kept up for about two hours, when it increased to a regular attack on all sides. Twice they succeeded in detaching a portion of the cattle from the main body, which were recaptured with considerable difficulty as the cattle so well understood the peculiar call of the Kaffirs that they did not seem to care about leaving their old masters.

We had only four wounded. We lost about 600 of our cattle, and the Kaffirs lost 160 killed. Their wounded they dragged away.

Jan. 15th, 1847. Two of the lightest men and two of the strongest horses were ordered to be selected for the purpose of conveying a despatch forward to King William's Town. I was one of the men selected. The distance was under 30 miles, but we were ordered to make two days of it as the horses were very weak. Prior to leaving, we each received 12 ounces of meal as rations for two days.

We started about 5 p.m. with orders to make 10 miles that evening and the remainder the following day. We were informed by the guide that we could not mistake the road as there was but one. Each of our guns was loaded and capped.

We made a good 10 miles, then halted for the night on good open ground. Neither of us ventured to go to sleep. We kept on the watch most intently; and fortunate we did as we had most foolishly neglected to put out our fire before darkness set in.

We were sitting on the ground, back to back, holding our horses—we had not removed the saddles—when an assegaie came and stuck in the ground within two yards of the place we were sitting. I jumped up and broke the shaft of the assegaie into pieces and put the blade into the wallet in front of my saddle. This was not the work of a minute, but it would prevent the assegaie being used again. We put the bridles on the horses and led them away from the fire in the very opposite direction to that we wanted to go—and it was also the direction from whence the assegaie had been thrown. We could tell by the direction of the shaft when it struck the ground.

After we had led them about 50 yards we got into the saddle, turned them sharply, around and galloped away in the opposite direction. We proceeded about a mile, when we again halted and dismounted. We reckoned it to be then about midnight. We rested there until daylight, when we again made a start.

We had got some 12 miles farther on our journey when, in passing through a straggling bush, two shots were fired and both went over our heads. We could hear them distinctly. When the casting nipple is not cut off, the ball makes a great whistling noise as it passes through the air.

Again we pushed on, and had arrived within three miles of our journey's end when another shot was fired. This time we were not so fortunate. My companion's horse received the ball in his shoulder. The charge of powder that had been used must have been small as the ball was not more than two inches embedded in the flesh and was easily removed.

We looked all around, but there was not a Kaffir to be seen. However, it would not do to stop there.

We must move, let it be ever so slowly; and at the rate the wounded horse was bleeding we knew he could not keep on his legs very long. We managed to stop the bleeding to a certain extent by plugging the hole with a piece of rag and pressing a tuft of grass upon it and leading him slowly along, while I kept a good look out all around.

At length we caught sight of a number of cattle grazing. I then knew we could not be far from the Station. When we came up with them I left my companion with the herds and galloped into King William's Town, which I reached in the evening.

Having delivered the despatch and reported about the man with the wounded horse being left on the road, a Farrier was sent to examine the horse, which was eventually brought in. And this finished my expedition across the Kei River. For hardships and privations endured on that campaign of only 25 days, I do not think the equal could be found in the history of modern warfare.

February 1st, 1847. King William's Town. Only a few months had elapsed since the first tent was pitched on this ground. At that time there was only the ruins of an old Mission Station which had, I believe, been destroyed by the Kaffirs during the War of 1834-35. Now streets were already being formed; huts rising in all directions; English and Dutch traders opening places of business for the sale of all kinds of articles and were doing a great trade as there was a large camp formed here. I had a fresh rig-out myself; bought a pair of boots, a shirt and a pair of leather crackers—trousers. When I got these things I felt quite a swell.

February 9th, 1847. With another Dragoon, I was sent with a despatch to Fort Stokes. On our road we came to a beautiful spring of water. so rarely are they to be met with that they are quite a treat. We dismounted, had a drink and sat on the ground a few minutes when two Kaffirs came and stretched themselves on the ground a few yards from us. They were both unarmed. I could only understand sufficient of their language as to make out that they were "friendly Kaffirs," although I had never heard of such Kaffirs at that time.

I had filled my pipe, and had left my knife and tobacco on the ground near my haversack for a minute only. When I went to pick them up, the knife was gone. I asked my companion if he had seen either of the Kaffirs pick it up, and he replied that he had not seen one of them move. I questioned them as well as I was able. No, they had not touched it—to which they both swore. However, the knife was gone.

We mounted our horses and was moving away when I happened to turn my head around and saw one of the Kaffirs stooping as if to pick something from the ground. I spun the horse round and was up to him in an instant. He had the knife in his hand. I should have chopped his arm off had he not immediately held out his hand to offer the knife to me, at the same time speaking in very intelligible English. He said he had not touched the knife at the time I asked him. His companion had raked some dirt over it with his foot as he lay on the ground when my back was turned and so covered it over so that I could not see it. On looking at the fellow more closely, I recognized him as a former servant of Mr. Moffat, the Missionary at Fort Beaufort, the notorious Jantze Pete.

On arriving at Fort Stokes I found that my leg was much swollen and very painful. The following morning we were ordered on to Fort Beaufort—38 miles—with another despatch. On reaching Fort Hare—26 miles—we rested two hours. I was in great pain when we started.

About four miles from Fort Beaufort we saw the remains of a waggon by the roadside that had recently been plundered by the Kaffirs—some of the friendly ones, most likely and afterwards set on fire. By the side of the waggon was the Hottentot driver, his head severed from his body and a few yards from it was the body of the little forelooper; and a short distance farther on,the body of an European hanging from a bush,most horribly mutilated.The oxen and contents of the waggon had been carried off by the Kaffirs. Such acts of barbarity were often committed by gangs of marauders who were too cowardly to join the main body of their countrymen but hung about the Colony to waylay and murder the unprotected.

On reaching Fort Beaufort I was lifted from my horse and taken into the Hospital. Both wounds were very bad and I was in a high state of fever. In a few hours I was delirious. Here I remained some time under the same Surgeon as before—Dr. Fouker—who said he would save the leg if possible, but of it at present he was doubtful as there were symptoms of mortification. However, plenty of cutting and burning again put it right. I certainly was most terribly tortured, but I believe not more than was actually necessary. I remained in Hospital and convalescent until late April.

Chapter Seventeen
Post & Express Riding

April 25th, 1847, With two others, I was sent with a despatch to Graham's Town (46 miles) with orders to rest two hours only at Koonap, which was about half way.

On reaching which we off-saddled the horses and let them have a roll on the grass, which refreshed them very much. We then "kneehalted" them, which is done by fastening the head to within about 18 inches of the knee by means of a *rhiem*—strip of hide—just allowing them sufficient length to enable them to reach the grass to eat. We then made a fire in order to prepare something for ourselves.

In the midst of the meal we missed one of the horses. Instantly we were on our feet, searching in all directions, but did not find the missing horse. What was to be done? Ah, that was the question! The despatch must go on; we could not leave behind the man who had lost his horse. We therefore decided that he should go with us on foot. But the next question was what was to become of his accoutrements and those belonging to his horse? We decided to hide the latter in the bush, and the former the man must carry with him.

We had not been started for many minutes when we heard several shots fired not very far from us. We hastened in the direction of the sound. I dismounted and caught sight of a Kaffir running along with the head collar in his hand belonging to the lost horse. I put a ball through his head without a moment's consideration.

A few minutes later we caught sight of a Dutch Burgher leading the missing horse by the foretop. The Burgher was one of a Detachment that was marching up country.

It appeared that they saw three Kaffirs with a horse. One was walking in front, unfastening the *rhiem* from the collar, which he had in his hand; the second was leading the horse by the foretop; the third was walking behind, driving the horse along toward a thick bush. Two of them were shot by the Burghers but the third escaped from them, but fell by a ball from me.

The saddle was got and put on, and we made another start. On passing through the bush leading from Koonap River we saw one of the Cape Mounted Rifles—a Hottentot—suspended from a tree near the roadside. His leather stock was round his neck, otherwise he was quite naked. The ground round about was strewn with fragments of letters. We took down the body, which was quite warm, and carried it into the bush and covered it with our hands as well as we could. What could have been the Kaffirs' motive for hanging him with his stock round his neck I could not imagine.

On our arrival at Graham's Town we reported what we had seen to the Brigade Officer, when it was at once ascertained that the Hottentot had left there that morning with a bag of letters for Fort Brown.

The people of the town were in a great state of excitement. Umkoa had given information that it was the intention of Pato—a very powerful Chief and a most bloodthirsty savage—to attack the town that night. The place was nearly destitute of fighting men as almost every available man had been summoned by Martial Law to take the field some time previous. 'Tis true there were only three of us newcomers, still they were glad of even this small addition to their strength.

We were detained in Graham's Town three days, and as there was no sign of any attack we were ordered to return to Fort Beaufort. Pato must either have changed his mind or the information was incorrect. The latter was not at all probable as Umkoa was invariably correct in the information he gave.

On reaching the Koonap bush, we found the body of the Hottentot again hanging from the same bush. The flesh had been cut from the legs and arms and the body most horribly mutilated. We did not deem it worth while to move the body again, as the Kaffirs would have been sure to drag it up again, and we had no means of digging a grave.

On reaching the Travellers' House at Koonap we gave information to the Proprietor, thinking he would send some of his Hottentot servants to bury the body. But he refused. We heard afterwards that he was on good terms with the Kaffirs and never interfered in any way in their little amusements. It is a most astonishing fact that he threw every obstacle in the way of furnishing provisions to the Troops passing his house. During the two years of that war he never left it, nor was he at any time molested by the Kaffirs, who called him "the good man." What his "goodness" consisted of, I cannot say, when hundreds of others were either murdered or had to fly for their lives. Question: Did he or had he supplied them with arms and ammunition in that isolated spot?

The day after I returned to Fort Beaufort I saw Mr. Moffat, and told him that his late servant, Jantze Pete, had gone to join his Tribe but the old gentleman would not believe it. He said he had given him one month's leave to go and see his friends, and when that time had expired he would return again. However, I ascertained when I enquired six months afterwards that Pete had not returned.

May 14th, 1847. I was sent with three others to Fort Hare, to be stationed until further orders as Post and Express Riders.

Previous to the breaking out of this war, the Lieutenant-Governor, Colonel Hare, wanted to build a Fort at this place; but Sandilla, the Paramount Chief of the Gaika Tribes, refused permission. A meeting was held on the spot and some very warm words ensued, but as I was not present I can only speak from hearsay. Sandilla spat in front of Colonel Hare and said:

"You have your men here and I have mine—let us fight for it."

Colonel Hare replied:

"I did not come here to fight. I have only my bodyguard with me."

The attitude of the Kaffirs was so threatening that the Artillery were ordered to load with cannister. And one of the men, whose duty it was to attend to the loading part of the business, put the powder in the wrong place, and the gun had to be up-ended to take the charge out again. The gunner was drunk and some of the gear was out of order. This incident was a well-known fact.

Several Missionaries had taken refuge in the Fort. I should like to know what had become of all the converts. Had they left one solitary Station standing where they used "to rush to the Chapel, even desert their cattle, when the Station bell rang for Prayers"?

June 14th, 1847. It was only to-day that I heard of the death of Captain Shepherd, the deaf Officer of the Royal Artillery. He had been murdered by one of his own men. Wheeler Long had shot him. He had persecuted that man most cruelly for a long time past, all because Long would not do what private work the Captain wanted done without payment. As I have said before he was, without exception, the greatest tyrant I ever met in the Service. Long was sentenced to be hung.

The number of narrow escapes I have had during the past month while on that most dangerous of all duties, post and express riding, were pretty numerous; but as there was such a sameness about them I will merely select one as an illustration.

One day I was, with two others, conveying a despatch from Fort Hare to King William's Town when we entered the dense bush on the banks of the Keiskama River. My horse became suddenly lame. I dismounted, when I found he had thrown a shoe and had been pricked with a thorn from a mimosa tree. Every Dragoon on service carried a spare set of shoes and nails and was supposed to know how to put on a shoe in case of emergency, using the small iron log as a hammer.

I soon set to work to replace the lost shoe. One of my companions remained with me, the other said he would take his horse and get a drink. The River was not more than 30 yards distant. Having succeeded in putting the shoe on sufficiently strong to carry me the remainder of the journey, we prepared to join our companion when suddenly we heard a noise which we knew by long experience was caused by tramping on the dry underwood of the bush.

Presently we caught sight of our companion. He was actually being dragged along by four Kaffirs. He was gagged by a piece of stick fastened across his mouth and his arms were fastened to his side. A Kaffir woman was leading his horse, and one of them was walking by his side, carrying his sword—this to prevent the sword making a noise by striking the ground. Two of the Kaffirs had guns, and each of the other two carried a bundle of assegaies. We had no fear of their guns so long as we were not within ten yards of them and the bush was too thick for them to do much with the assegaies, still the latter was the most dangerous for us.

Our arrangements were soon made. We decided to settle the two with the assegaies. They were not more than 15 yards from us when we both fired. Two of the Kaffirs fell, both shot through the head. The other two shouted, "*Mar Wo, Rooi Badjies*" Oh, dear Red Coats.

One of the survivors stooped down to seize one of the bundles of assegaies, but my companion rushed forward and drove his sword through the Kaffir's body. The other got away. The woman with the horse had bolted when the shots were fired.

We released our companion. The affair had given him a bit of a fright, but not so much as one might imagine. He said he was in the act of drinking at the Riverside when the Kaffirs pounced on him, so suddenly that he had no time to defend himself or call for help before he was gagged and fastened. He said he made as much noise as he could in passing through the bush in order that we might hear him. He knew that that was his only chance.

We carried the two bundles of assegaies and the gun belonging to the dead Kaffirs to King William's Town and left them with a report of the affair at the brigade Office. We were told that we should receive something in the shape of a reward for the arms we ad captured, but the reward was like the back rations -not allowed. On our return journey, four days after, in passing through the same bush we saw the three bodies had been removed. On reaching Fort Hare we found that a Division had reached there consisting of 50 Dragoons, 120 Cape Mounted Rifles, 250 of the 45th Regiment, 50 Kaffir Police and a few Burghers. I was ordered to join this Division. Our destination was the Amatola Mountains in pursuit of the Chief Sandilla,who was reported to have again taken up his quarters there with about 1,000 of his Tribe.

One of the Officers,Captain P. M.Bunbury, 7th Dragoon Guards, with whom I had always been a great favourite, wished me to go with him as his servant.But everyone knew he was a most hasty-tempered man and I was spoken of as being equally as bad, and Captain Bunbury had had more men for servants than any Officer in the Regiment. However, I consented to serve him on this Campaign.

The following day the Division left the Fort and reached the thick bush on the Keiskama River at sunset. Here we remained until midnight, when we again saddled up and moved on in two Divisions; the Cavalry in one, the Infantry in the other as the latter could take a much shorter route than the Cavalry on account of the difficulty of getting the horses through the bush by that route.

At daybreak the Cavalry reached a small plateau. The Infantry had not arrived. No time could be lost as we could not possibly remain there many minutes before we should have been seen by the Scouts of the enemy. We were then about two miles from Sandilla's Kraal. Accordingly the Cavalry advanced as quick as the nature of the ground would allow.

In consequence of having my Master's pack horse to lead, my place was in the rear of the Troops, that is between the Troops and the Rear Guard. We were going along at a good swinging pace when suddenly my pack saddle turned around, and away went both the saddle bags under the horse's belly. The Rear Guard, contrary to all orders, did not stop to assist me but galloped on and left me alone by myself. Certainly they were only Hottentots of the Cape Mounted Rifles that formed the Rear Guard and I suppose knew no better, but had the Rear Guard been Dragoons and had left one of these Colonial "pets" in a similar position they would assuredly have been tried by Court Martial and severely punished.

Foolishly, I dismounted and endeavoured to put the saddle right when several Kaffirs pounced on me. What a pleasant situation, to be sure—no arms to defend myself with, and each of them with a bundle of assegaies! I never felt so certain of death as at that moment, yet I can positively say my feeling was not fear. I had no time to be frightened. In one moment the bags were off the saddle and they were endeavouring to unfasten the straps.

Suddenly they all jumped and disappeared in the bush. Their quick ear had caught the sound of the Infantry coming. One of the Kaffirs threw an assegaie which just drew blood from my left shoulder.

From beginning to end, this little affair was not more than three minutes. Had the Infantry marched by the route expected, I should never have seen them. With their assistance the saddle was put right, and I remained with them until we joined the Cavalry at Burns Hill Missionary Station, which had been left by the Missionary in charge of the converted Kaffirs, and within 12 hours of his departure they plundered the Station and set fire to it. Throughout the War I did not meet with one Missionary who had sufficient confidence in his converts to remain with them, yet I have no doubt but some of them had thrilling tales to tell the old ladies at Exeter Hall.

On reaching the Cavalry, I found that half of them had been sent forwards to Sandilla's Kraal, distant about half a mile. The order was given that Sandilla was not on any account to be shot, but was to be taken prisoner. But the alarm had been given and before the party got to the Kraal the Kaffirs rushed out and made for the nearest bush. Several men had a very good chance of shooting the Chief, but they were unable to take him prisoner. He made his escape into the bush.

About 40 most wretched looking cattle were found in the Kraal, which were taken possession of by the Troops and brought back to Burns Hill and then given over in charge of the Kaffir Police. The latter was, I believe, the most useless body of men I ever saw. All they were fit for was to lower the store of ammunition.

After handing over the cattle we expected to have so breakfast. I was as busy as a nailer getting my Master some chocolate ready.

"Mind and don't forget yourself," said he. "You will find plenty in the bag where you got the chocolate. Don't be afraid of it. Let me have a slice of German when the chocolate is ready. I'm in no hurry."

A good job he was not in a hurry, as at that moment the Camp alarm sounded. The Kaffir Police had let the Kaffirs take the cattle from them, and the former were throwing away their ammunition as fast as they could. As it happened, there was a certain number of the Cape mounted Rifles were to go with the Kaffir Police but had not yet started. But on the alarm being given they jumped into the saddle and succeeded in recapturing the cattle and bringing them back.

In the meantime the chocolate had been upset and all the things had been bundled into the saddle bags, and we were on the move again. A great number of Kaffirs were seen passing along a ridge, and very shortly after another lot was seen coming from another direction. The Officer in Command of the Kaffir Police informed the Commanding Officer that the Kaffirs were all making for the Blind Drift of the Keiskama River, where it was expected we should cross, and the longer we remained here the more we should have to contend with when we got there.

The order was given to push on at once to Fort Hare— 36 miles—and the very worst road in Kaffir land. In fact, it is my belief without exaggeration the Cavalry of the British Army never led horses over such ground as we traversed that day in the Amatola Mountains.

The Kaffirs did not let us get far before they opened fire. The whole of the Cavalry were dismounted. The Kaffirs appeared determined that we should not take away their only chance of subsistence without a struggle. They were gathering around us in thousands. By their number it was quite evident that the whole of the Gaika Tribes had again located themselves in those fastnesses.

In their attempts to get the cattle, many of them were bayonetted by the men of the 45th Regiment, and were also shot down by hundreds. Our spies reported that the main body of the enemy had gone to line the bush leading to the Blind Drift, consequently our route was changed to another place where the River was fordable, but more dangerous on account of the steepness of the banks on both sides of the River. (Keiskama.)

We got along very slowly indeed. The cattle were the most wretched animals I ever saw. It was not for their value they were taken. It was to show them that the Government was determined to punish them; also, having got possession of them, we should keep them no matter what sacrifice of life might be in so doing.

The whole of the Infantry excepting the Rear Guard crossed the River first. The water was up to their shoulders. How ever the Cavalry got across has ever been a mystery to me. Several horses were shot in the river because as they were struggling no other horses could be got near them until several shots were fired at them and their bodies went floating down the River.

I had two horses—one I was riding and the pack horse I leading. I have some faint recollection of struggling in the bush on the bank and of eventually going head over heels with the two horses into the river, where I was floundering about for some time before I could get up the opposite bank. However I managed to do so at last.

Shortly after I saw my Master. He asked me if I was wet. I told him I was certainly somewhat damp as I had been under the water twice in the River when I fell down the bank struggling with the horses. He said:

"Never mind; you are no worse than I am."

I don't believe I was, as he was rather short in stature and the water must have come quite up to his chin in walking through it. When those of the enemy who had gone to the Blind Drift found their mistake, they were very soon after us and came up with us about two miles from the River, and as the bush was not so dense we made a stand.

The Kaffirs boldly advanced. I never saw such slaughter. Here we had one Officer and one Private killed and several wounded, all of the 45th Regiment. The Infantry was nearly exhausted. They had been 15 hours marching, 11 of them under a burning sun with a greatcoat and blanket on their back, and nothing to eat or drink except the little they might have snatched up with their hands on passing through the River. The last 8 miles had been a complete running fight. As the bush was somewhat thin, we halted about every 50 yards and gave them a volley. Still on they came, not the least daunted.

Several of the 45th fell from exhaustion and were lifted on to the Dragoons' horses. I should think there was not less than 30 so mounted, wounded and exhausted together.

The Kaffirs saw this and did all in their power to take advantage of it. We had to pass through a small ravine, and here the Kaffirs completely surrounded us. I am sure there must have been quite 200 killed and wounded within 100 yards of this place.

Having reached the top of a small hill where there was but little bush, a Council of War was held; then the fact became known that nearly one-half of our force was without ammunition. The wounded and exhausted lay about on the ground; in fact, the whole of the Infantry were nearly done up. As I have said before, there was no conveyance for the wounded in those. How many lives were sacrificed during that War for the want of it! More than one case came under my personal observation.

The Kaffirs did not venture beyond the ravine before mentioned. The ground was too open. They had not forgotten meeting with the Dragoons on the Gwanga Flats in 1846. They said they are not afraid of any number of *Rooi Badjies*——Red Coats— in the bush, but they would not face the *Pearl Rooi Badjies*—Horse Red Coats—with the *croote mess* —big knife—on the plain again if they could help it.

It was estimated by the Council of War that we were nearly surrounded by 15,000 Kaffirs. Had they boldly closed in on us, not one of us could possibly have escaped. At length it was decided that 8 of the lightest men—volunteers—and the same number of the strongest horses should be selected to make a dash for Fort Hare—5 miles—for ammunition and reinforcements.

The men and horses were selected without creating the least suspicion among the enemy, although the main body of them was within 200 yards of us. At a given signal the men jumped into the saddle and away they went. I heard one of the Officers say: "If only one man reaches the Fort we shall be all right, but I am doubtful about it." And so were we all.

When the Kaffirs saw them gallop off, they began to yell like fury. They well knew where the men were going and what was their errand. They rushed toward a small ravine to intercept them, but the Dragoons were too smart for them.

The next thing to be done was to examine the ammunition in our possession, when it was found that there was an average of only three rounds per man and one in the barrel. There was no necessity to caution the men to be careful of it. It was too precious to be thrown away, and it was quite evident that it would be dark before any the messengers could return with a fresh supply. And another most important matter was that it would not do to let the Kaffirs hold possession of the ravine after dark or they would have us in a trap.

20 Dragoons on foot and 50 of the 45th were ordered to dislodge them and hold possession of the ravine until reinforcement should arrive. Only one volley was fired, and the remainder were driven out with sword and bayonet.

At length the party returned, bringing with them as much ammunition as they could carry. During the time they were away we had only two or three wounded, and two of those had died who had been wounded in the early part of the day. A drink of water might have saved both of them, but it was not to be had. Not less than 300 of the enemy could have been killed at this place.

When we prepared to start we had the greatest difficulty in getting the cattle to move. They must have been nearly starved when we took them. We had not proceeded far when we found the Kaffirs had taken up a position in our front, and when we approached they made a dash for the cattle. Amid the noise of the firing and the yells of the Kaffirs, the cattle appeared to go wild and we lost some of them; but just at that time a reinforcement arrived and they drove the Kaffirs before them.

Volley after volley was poured into them, after which we were allowed to reach the Fort in peace about midnight, after 66 hours of marching and fighting without a particle of food and only one chance of a mouthful of water—I had two or three more than I wanted when I was floundering about in the River. The suffering of the wounded for want of water was very great.

On reaching the Fort we found that plenty of food had been prepared for us and each man received one pint of wine; and within one hour most of us had forgotten our troubles and was fast asleep.

Some time during the night I was aroused by hearing some one enquiring for me. The thought struck me directly "I guess they want me for duty," but I had made up my mind they should find me first. I felt that I had had quite enough duty during the last 66 hours.

Presently I recognized the voice of my Master. I had forgotten all about him. I need scarcely say he was somewhat angry, but I knew he was hungry so I made every allowance for his anger. Yet he was not so angry as one might imagine. He had had a glass of sherry and a biscuit with one of his brother Officers, so he told me, and he only wanted to know if I had looked after the horses. Yes, I had watered and fed them and would give them another feed at daybreak. My Master appeared satisfied and said:

"Never mind me, but don't neglect the horses."

I could not but sincerely apologize for my neglect, and offered to get him anything from the saddle bags he might desire. He said:

"No, I do not want anything now, but will you make me a drop of coffee about 4 o'clock?"

The following day the Cavalry returned to Fort Beaufort, and I resumed my duties as post and express rider.

Chapter Eighteen
A Journey into the Bush

July 4th, 1847. This being my birthday and also my day off duty, I thought I would take a little recreation. Having plenty of powder and shot, I borrowed a gun from one of my Hottentot friends and, accompanied by two others, went a little way along the bank of the River in search of peafowl, wild duck or any thing else in the shape of sport.

I was exceedingly fortunate, as I got as much game in about three hours as the Totties could well carry. When returning, I could not resist the opportunity offered for another shot. I fired and the bird flew apparently only a few yards. One of the Totties followed to pick it up, and myself and the other walked slowly on to the Fort.

We had returned some time when, there being no sign of the Tottie making his appearance, his companion, with several others, went in search of him. They returned at dusk without having found him. The Kaffirs had got him, that was quite evident.

The following morning I was ordered to attend the Garrison Office and was severely reprimanded by the Fort Adjutant for going beyond the Fort Boundary. A party of Hottentots was sent out in search of the missing man. They discovered the body about one mile from the Fort.

He had been stripped of his clothing and fastened to the ground close to a large ant hill, on his back, by his hands and feet. He had then been rubbed over with honey, after which the ant hill was broken open, when thousands of great African black ants would rush out and at once make for the body, which they soon eat into by the ears, eyes, nostrils and other parts. It must be a most horrible death. The remains were brought in and interred the same evening. The poor

Tottie! I was very sorry, as I felt that I was to a certain extent the cause of his death.

Those who have not seen or read of the African black ant would scarcely credit how large they are and the size of the hills they make. Once out of curiosity I measured one. It was over three feet in height and eight feet in diameter; and I have heard that many are a great deal larger.

July 20th, 1847. I received a letter from the Officer whom I had served on the recent short campaign, asking if I would come to him as his servant. I consented and left Fort Hare for that purpose. I cannot say willingly, as I knew I had a very hot-headed gentleman to deal with;and I was not one of the most amiable of tempers myself at times and knew as much about the duties of an Officer's servant as a child. At my request, the engagement was conditioned, namely, I was to serve him for one month, at the end of which, if either was not satisfied, I should be allowed to return to my duty as before.

At the expiration of the time mentioned I found that I had got on very well, although I had by chance heard that one of the other Officers should say that "me and my Master were well matched." However, I consented to remain as servant.

August 27th, 1847. My Master obtained six days leave of absence and the same for me to accompany him on a short shooting excursion to Leu Fontein, a distance of about 12 miles from Fort Beaufort— Colony side.

We put up at a African Hotel. Such places were to be found in all parts of the Colony, from 20 to 40 miles apart, the proprietors of which were invariably large cattle and sheep breeders. There was also a small Commissariat Store here in charge of Mr. Moffat,late of my Regiment,who had been discharged, having lost one arm. He was also the husband of the "Female Sailor" before mentioned in this book.

The first day that we went out, we shot more wild duck and water hen than we could carry on our horses. We returned in the evening, in the course of which the proprietor informed my Master that most likely he would be able to show him some lions before he retired, but he must promise not to molest them in any way. The promise was given.

I spent an hour or two in the hut with Mr. and Mrs. Moffat, listening to her adventures as a sailor; and by what I saw during my visit I was of opinion that it would have been much better for her husband if her sex had never been discovered.

My Master was on the point of retiring for the night when one of the Fingo herds came in and reported that the lions were there. We went outside of the house and there, sure enough, was four lions—two large and two small ones—drinking at a small stream not more than 80 yards from the house. My Master sadly wanted to have a shot at them, but was reminded of his promise. The proprietor said that for some months past these lions had been seen repeatedly drinking at the same spring, and no one had been allowed to fire at them. My Master said:

"If Gordon Cumming was here he would not let such a chance pass him, I know."

The moon was shining brightly at the time and we could see them distinctly. At night there was a great number of sheep near the house only guarded by dogs, yet the lions never disturbed them.

We were out the following morning by daylight with one guide and four beaters, all Fingoes. As I have before remarked, these people were at one time a very powerful tribe of Kaffirs, so we were told. If it was so, they must have been a very different stamp of men to what they are now; I mean their pluck. They did not appear to me to have a particle of that commodity about them; in short, they were the most abject cowards I ever met.

After we had been out a few hours we came in sight of a very large deer called by the natives a Koodoo. My Master fired two shots at him, but he got away. All the Fingoes except one had been sent on to prepare food for us or the deer would not have got off so cheap. However, it was not for long, as shortly afterwards the Fingoe called out that he had found the "spoor" of the wounded deer, also a tree marked with blood where he had been rubbing his body. We continued to follow the spoor, but unfortunately, it was in the direction opposite to that where the Fingoes had been sent. The one who remained with us, who spoke Dutch, told me that, and I told my Master, who said:

"Never mind the grub. There's some biscuit and a flask of sherry in my saddle pocket. We must make shift with that tonight. If we don't come up with them, they'll and their way home right enough."

We kept on the track of the wounded deer until dark, when we made a good fire. My Master made his supper off some biscuits and sherry, and a portion came to my share together with part of a water hen which I frizzled on the fire, after which we had a nap.

The spoor was easily found the next morning. These people can tell by examining a spoor how long a time has elapsed since the cattle passed, whether they were driven fast or slow, by a native or by a white man, near what district they had been feeding, and many other things which enable them to trace lost cattle, that would puzzle a European.

During the morning we came across a drove of springbok. In my opinion they are the prettiest specie of the deer I ever saw.

In the afternoon we came up with the wounded Koodoo. He was standing under a tree and appeared nearly exhausted. One shot settled him. The Fingoe wanted to know what my Master was going to do with it. He was the largest deer I ever saw; his antlers were an immense length. My Master decided to have him skinned and the carcass sent in to Fort Beaufort. The horns he would keep for himself, but the skin came to my share, which I sold the next evening for 30 shillings to a gentleman staying at the Hotel.

The following day we took a different direction, and were out about seven hours. Between us we shot 4 jackals, 1 wolf,

34 water hens, 2 swans, 13 geese and 26 ducks. My Master was an excellent shot with either fowling piece or pistol. The last day my Master gave me to do as I pleased, so I decided to do a little shooting on my own account. I got a Hottentot to accompany me, as I preferred a Tottie to a Fingoe at any time. If accompanied by the former, he has always got some wild, improbable or laughable story to tell; whereas the latter is sullen, morose, or what I should call "pigish." We were not out more than five hours, and we brought home as much game as we could carry; and I was quite ready for my dinner.

After that I went off for a few hours fishing. My Tottie companion of the morning went with me to show me where there was plenty of fish. There is no mistake, I never saw such fishing in my life. I caught over 20 splendid fish within one hour, and returned to the Hotel at dark. I gave the Totty a shilling for his trouble, but it was a long time before I could prevail on him to take it. He said he did not want any thing for his trouble—would rather not take anything —as I was such a *banya mooi baas*—very good master.

I was called up pretty early the following morning. My Master said he could not sleep for thinking about the fish I brought home the night previous. He was very fond of angling. He said he must go and have a couple of hours before he started. I went with him to show him the place, but he had more than two hours; he stayed there until near the evening, when we prepared to return to Fort Beaufort.

Just previous to starting, my Totty companion of the day previous brought me a very pretty gourd.

It was late when we reached Fort Beaufort and we were a day beyond our time, but nothing was said about it. The gourd that had been given me I gave to another Totty of the opposite gender.

Chapter Nineteen
Against the Amatola Kaffirs

October 7th, 1847. Went with my Master on a four days patrol with 40 Dragoons and one Company of the 6th Regiment into the Amatola, for the purpose of destroying huts and crops belonging to the Kaffirs who had located themselves in those fastnesses.

In the evening we came to a small, newly constructed village. There was about 20 huts, but no cattle. The Kaffirs had by some means got information of our approach and made their escape into the bush. They must have been there some considerable time as their crops were in a forward state, which were all destroyed by the Troops and the huts set on fire.

At night, as we were not troubled with any camp equipage, each man made himself as comfortable as he could under a bush. About midnight the Kaffirs, no doubt thinking we were more comfortable than we had any right to be, began firing at us and calling to us to know why we had come there and destroyed their crops as they were friendly Kaffirs. If they were such they had a peculiar way of showing their friend ship—or did they try to convince us by coming and offering the right hand? I expect they thought they could show it best by firing at us from the bush.

However, their shots done us no harm, and by daybreak all was quiet. What my Master subsisted on, I cannot say. I know that I prepared nothing for him except a pot of coffee. This and two small biscuits was all he had since he left the Fort.

October 8th, 1847. The Troops moved toward Fort Cox. A heavy thunderstorm came on. We were making our way up the side of the mountain, and the ground was so slippery that we had great difficulty in leading the horses and keeping them on their feet. After some hours hard labour we reached a small ridge, and as it was utterly impossible to proceed any farther while the rain lasted we were obliged to stand there and hold our horses.

The Infantry succeeded in reaching a ridge above us and in that comfortable position we had to remain the whole of the following night, and to make it more pleasant, we had nothing to eat and (were) not allowed to make any fires as we were in a very bad position.

Master did not appear to be in any trouble about having no food. Some time during the night he said:

"Don't forget to make some coffee as soon as it is daylight."

October 9th, 1847. The rain did not cease for some time after sunrise, but then the sun came out strong which soon dried the ground sufficient to enable us to reach a small plateau covered with a straggling bush. Here we halted and fastened our horses to the bush. We then stripped off a portion of our clothing and hung them up to dry, after which I set to work to make a fire.

Previous to leaving the Fort on the 7th inst. every man had been served out with 4 lbs of beef, and by this time what there was left of that quantity had become a little the worse for keeping, probably this was caused by the mode of conveyance, which was thus:

The Cavalry carried the meat in their mess tins. The latter was carried in the horse's nosebag, slung to the off side of the saddle in close proximity to the body of the horse. The motion of the horse caused the mess tin to act as a kind of sieve, as we invariably found on opening the nosebag the corn to be particularly clean as the whole of the dust and dirt had sifted into the mess tin which contained the meat.

The Infantry carried their meat rolled up in their greatcoat, which was strapped on their back; but when wearing the greatcoat they were obliged to carry it the best way they could or throw it away which they were often obliged to do. From this any one may form a pretty good idea of the amount of trouble that was bestowed in conducing to the comforts of the soldier in those "Good Old Times." I have heard it said "the hungry dog will eat dirty meat." Yes, and so will a hungry man.

It might be said that my Master was not so badly provided for and that I might by chance fall in for a little of his provender, which was most true, as nearly the whole of his store fell to my share on this occasion —on the same principle as I was once accosted by a country clown at a public house where I was billetted, asking me to have some beer: "Here, sup, sojer; I can't drink any more."

I carried a small saddle pocket fastened on each side of my saddle. One contained a few toilet articles and a flask of brandy; the other a roast duck some biscuits and a flask of sherry. But the duck was rather too high and my Master desired me to throw it away, but I am sorry to say I was guilty of disobedience of orders. The biscuit had become somewhat tainted also, being in such close proximity to the duck. The biscuits shared the same fate as the duck so far as my Master was concerned. However, I procured a biscuit for my Master from one of the men in exchange for a portion of the aforesaid duck. I fancy I can smell it now.

After our refreshment we went on again, and just before sunset we came in sight of another newly built village. The Cavalry advanced at a gallop. The Kaffirs rushed out of the huts into the bush, from which they fired a few shots that did no harm to any of us.

There was about 20 goats in the Kraal, which we took possession of. We then began to set fire to the huts, and 4 Kaffirs bolted from one of them, each with a bundle of assegaies. They were all shot. Those who had escaped from the huts were met in the bush by the Infantry and very few of them escaped; after which the Infantry again joined the Cavalry and as the ground was pretty good and free from bush, it was decided to remain there for the night.

The moon shone bright and we were allowed to make fires, and in a very short time we were revelling in the luxuries afforded by the late capture. Six goats were killed and divided among us, and the same number for the Infantry; and, having found some Kaffir corn in one of the huts, we got on very well.

I cannot say my Master fared so well, as all he had during the day was a small piece of biscuit and a pot of coffee. Still, he appeared wonderfully contented. He would say, "If you get a chance, make me a drop of coffee." When he had got that, I had only to fill his pipe and give him a light and he was satisfied.

October 10th, 1847. At daybreak we received information that a large number of Kaffirs without cattle had located themselves near to the Amatola Basin. The Infantry moved off at once, and the Cavalry about one hour after. About midday we heard some sharp firing, and gradually the sound came nearer. It was quite evident that the Infantry were retiring. The Kaffirs' bullets came whistling over our heads. The bush was too thick for Cavalry to act, consequently we were dismounted. One-third of the men was left in charge of the horses, and the remainder advanced to join the Infantry, who had been obliged to retire as the Kaffirs were too many for them.

When we reached them, the whole advanced, and the Kaffirs were driven in front like a flock of sheep. At this time their ammunition was getting low; in fact it had been reported by our spies that some of the Tribes were entirely without any. The assegaie was utterly useless in the bush except at close quarters— and that they dreaded.

The whole force advanced, followed by the men leading the horses. On nearing the village the bush became much thinner, and we had three men wounded with the assegaies which began to fly about. The horses were brought up. The Cavalry mounted and galloped into the village, and the Kaffirs making for the thick bush.

We found about 40 huts, but not a soul in one of them. The land all around was cultivated. The former were set on fire and the crops destroyed as much as possible in the time that could be spared for that purpose, after which the remainder of the goats were killed. I never had thought that goat's flesh was so nice. Certainly it was rather tough, but what is that when one is hungry? Hunger—why, it is the finest sauce in the world. I have proved that many times.

As our position was not quite so good as on the night previous and having a few wounded, we were obliged to put every man on duty, two hours on and four off. The saddle turned upside down would form a most excellent resting place for one's head and shoulders, the fans of the saddle keeping the wind off most beautifully.

Of course the wounded were cared for. We had a Surgeon with us, but I know his stock of medical comforts was not very extensive as I heard him tell my Master, when speaking of the wounded. These were his words:

"I have only got my instrument case, a few small pieces of rag, a piece of plaster, my pipe and tobacco pouch."

Which was invariably the full extent of the medical comforts carried for the wounded. My Master gave what brandy and sherry he had to be divided among the wounded.

October 11th, 1847. At daylight we prepared to return to Fort Beaufort. We had a sad job with the wounded. Two of them were so exhausted they could not sit on a horse. Branches of trees were got and litters were made for them but two of them died before we reached the Fort.

October 15th, 1847. A Private of the Regiment was flogged for theft. Another of those brutal exhibitions took place which would be a disgrace to any nation which boasts far less of its enlightenment and Christianity than England.

The number of men I have seen flogged during my career of 23 years and 8 months in the Service would not be less than 100. I have closely watched the career of many of the recipients of this degrading punishment, and I can safely say that I never knew not even one that it made any improvement in, either his moral character or as a soldier. But on the other hand, how many a good and brave soldier has been lost to the Army through the brutal punishment of the lash, inflicted for some offence committed at the commencement of his career as a soldier. I will give one case as an illustration.

In 1843 a young Soldier of the 7th Dragoon Guards received four dozen lashes with the "Thief's Cat" for theft. As I have already given an account of the crime and punishment,there is no necessity for me to enter on that part of the subject again. From this degradation he never recovered. He lingered in the Regiment until 1848; and during that time there was not one Officer or Soldier in the Regiment who did not believe him innocent of the crime for which he had been so severely punished.Everything that kindness could suggest was done for him, but to no purpose, and they were obliged to discharge him. He left the army a broken-down old man at the age of twenty-five.

One man I saw flogged, when the last lash was inflicted, turned round to the Commanding Officer and said: "Give me my discharge and I will take the same number over again." I have heard several exclaim after the last lash had been given,"Domino!"

Our legislators are of opinion that the Army could not get on without the lash,particularly in wartime. Don't believe it. There were many ways even then of punishing the bad soldier without making him worse than a brute. Did it never occur to the minds of those in command how easy it would be, during the Kaffir War for instance when engaged in bush fighting, for the man who had been flogged to shoot the author of his degradation? I have often thought of that since the death of Captain Bambrick in 1846— the best friend I ever had.

Chapter Twenty
Camp Life

November 4th, 1847. I was sent with my Master to join a Division under the command of Sir George Berkeley that was encamped on Committees Flats. And it was here I made the discovery that grooming four horses, washing my Master's linen, cooking for him and being his valet, was rather more than I could manage and was obliged to come to some understanding in reference to the quantity of linen he was to use weekly.

It was finally settled that he was not to use more than a complete change twice each week. Many a laugh have I had at the thought of my position— groom, cook, valet and washerman. We invariably had words on changing days about the buttons of his shirts. Sometimes he would say:

"Why, there is not a single button on this shirt. I can't wear it like this. Do try and put some on, that's a good fellow."

I would reply:

"I cannot help it, Sir. I have got no buttons, and if I had I have no needle and thread."

Before we left the Fort my Master several times told me to be sure and get everything I wanted, but I never once thought of needles and thread such as would be used for sewing on buttons. I certainly had got needles and thread, but not of the size suitable for the purpose required.

My Master would endeavour to persuade me to try and borrow the necessary articles. He would say:

"When you want anything you have not got, don't you try and borrow it of your comrades?"

I replied:

"I do not, Sir, When I want anything I have not got I do

without it, and you must do the same. I never borrow."

Eventually he got a reel of cotton, a needle and a few buttons from a brother officer of the 45th, so after that there was no excuse about buttons, although I was about as handy at such a job as an elephant.

One day my Master said to me:

"Adams, I have been talking to Captain Tench of the 45th. He tells me his servant starches his shirts for him most beautiful, in fact equal to any woman. Don't you think you might be able to starch one for me occasionally?"

This was entirely a new line of business. However, I said:

"I have no doubt what you say, Sir, is quite true, but this is the first time I ever aspired to the honour of washing for an Officer, and you must bear in mind, Sir, that you have four horses for me to look after. Captain Tench has but one and that barely worthy the name of a horse, therefore his servant has plenty of time to do things for his Master which I cannot do for you." At all events, not wishing to be beaten by a brother flunkey, I said: "Well, Sir, if you will get the starch and the iron, I will see what I can do."

My Master was quite elated at the idea of sporting a starched shirt in Camp. Away he went off to Captain Tench, and shortly after returned with a packet of starch in one hand and a flat iron in the other.

"Here you are. When will you have a try? Captain Tench's servant is coming over to give you a little instruction. Oh, here he comes."

I took the starch and the iron. Better that I had never seen either starch or iron. Both me and my Master would have been one shirt the richer. Having washed two shirts for my Master and one for myself, I prepared the starch in the following manner:

I first put a large camp kettle of boiling water into a bathtub, then the half-pound packet of starch, and after stirring it up well I put in the three shirts, thinking I might as well have a starched shirt as there was plenty of starch.

I stirred them well around with a stick, after which I put them on a bush to dry. I then set to work to heat the iron, and left it in the fire while I went to water the horses. On my return, having satisfied myself that the iron was hot—for I had taken hold of it and was very soon glad to drop it again—I then went to get one of the shirts, which I found standing bolt upright against the bush on which I had hung it. It was like a wooden shirt.

"Hello," said I. "There must be some mistake here."

Fortunately, memory came to my aid. What a blessing it is to those who possess a good one! I had some faint recollection of seeing my mother sprinkle the linen with water during some part of the process. I accordingly applied some water, then I tried to rub the shirt soft, but could not succeed by any means in reducing it to the proper state of pliability.

However I thought that would be of very little consequence, so I spread a horse blanket on the ground, not thinking for one moment whether the unevenness of the surface would make any difference. I laid out the shirt as even as the starch and the nature of the ground would allow, then seized hold of the iron, but not with the naked hand this time—and clapped it on the shirt.

One fizz, a little smoke, and it was in a blaze. Yes, and in less than one minute there was only part of one sleeve left—for hot climates these articles are made exceedingly thin. Then quite naturally I came to the conclusion that the iron was rather too hot, so I laid it aside for a minute or two while I shook the ashes of the defunct shirt from the blanket and again spread it on the ground.

I then tried the iron on my own shirt, and in less than two seconds I had burned a hole through it the exact size of the iron. About this time I heard my Master call out:

"Adams, I wish you would not be burning rags so near my hut. The wind blows the smoke right in here and it is very unpleasant."

Yes, I thought to myself, there will be a jolly shine presently about the rags. A few minutes after he came out and I heard him say to himself:"What ever is the fellow up to now?" When he came a little nearer he said:

"Why, anybody can smell that you are burning that shirt."

I was on my knees at the moment, holding up and looking at the hole I had made in my own shirt.

"Yes, Sir," I replied."And I have burned a great blister on my hand."

"And serve you right," said he. "You stupid fool, whatever are you doing, burning the horse blanket like that?"

"I beg your pardon,Sir"I continued."It is not the blanket but one of your shirts. I have been rather unfortunate with this one" holding up the fragment of the sleeve, which was all there was left of it—"but I will endeavour to be more careful with the other."

He enquired:"Where is the other?"

I pointed it out, standing against the bush stiff as a board.

I cannot remember all the names my Master applied to me, but I know that "ass" and "stupid fool" were among the mildest.And lastly he told me I was a greater fool than he ever took me for, and it was a great pity that when I put the shirts into the boiling starch I had not put myself in with them.

At this moment Captain Tench and several other Officers came up and laughed heartily at the blunder I had made, and began giving me some instructions what to do the next time I made the attempt. Tench roared with laughter when I told him I had put the whole of the packet of starch in at once. Captain Tench told my Master that he had sent his servant over expressly to give me the necessary instructions. If he did, I did not remember it.

My Master was very angry, not at the loss of the shirt, though his wardrobe at this time was exceedingly limited, but at the jokes that would be passed on him by the Officers in the Camp, every one of whom by this time knew of the mess I had made. However, I made up my mind not to have any more to do with the laundry business, at all events not in the fancy line. How many times I was obliged to wash the two shirts that were not entirely destroyed before I could get the starch out of them I cannot tell. Within 24 hours it became a regular by-word in the Camp. "How are you off for starch?" or "After you for a rub of the flat iron."

Some of them carried the joke a little too far. Among that number was the Commissariat Officer, and I believe that gentleman and my Master came to blows over it, as I found the latter one morning, when I took him his usual tot of coffee, bathing his face, and there were slight symptoms of a black eye.

Eventually the chaffing ruffled my Master's temper to such an extent that we could not agree, and I requested that he get another servant. He said he did not wish me to leave him, but he was tired of being perpetually humbugged by certain Officers, whom he named, always chaffing him about starch.

One day the flunkey who had been sent to give me instructions ventured to call after me:

"Buck, how are you off for starch?"

I went after him like a shot. He ran in between two of the Officers' tents. I came up with him and hit him once or twice, and we both tumbled over the tent ropes. He then bolted into one of the tents, me after him. I fell over a bath-tub and went butt up against an Officer who was sitting on a small camp stool at a table, writing. We all three went rolling on the ground together.

As soon as the Officer gained his feet he ran out of the tent and I looked around for my opponent, but he had made his escape by the opposite door of the tent. Almost immediately I was taken possession of by the Guard and marched off, a prisoner, to the Camp Guard Tent; and about an hour after I was taken before the Officer Commanding the Camp and my crime was read to me as follows:

"Fighting in Camp, making forcible entry into the tent of Captain Tench, knocking down that Officer and breaking an inkstand and a camp stool."

The crime was of quite sufficient gravity to hang a man six times over, but the Commanding Officer knew pretty well what was the origin of the whole affair, and my Master having arranged with Captain Tench in reference to the breakages, I was liberated with a caution. And from this time on there was no more chaffing about starch and flat iron.

The hardest job of all in Camp was cooking, especially when one's stock of utensils was not more than me and my Master possessed between us; namely, one camp kettle, one saucepan minus lid and handle, one piece of iron hoop bent to answer the purpose of a gridiron, one tin pot and the blade of an old shovel. The three latter articles were my property.

I am perfectly satisfied there was not one Officer in the Camp had such a stock of the good things of life as my Master. And he was not a little vain when letting his friends see and partake of them. If I was laughed at for my failure in the laundry line, there was no one in the Camp who could compete with me in the gastronomic art; yet I was never cook to a Hotel or a cook shop but indebted to my mother for what little knowledge I possessed in the culinary art.

Some people might ask what use could I make of the blade of a shovel in cooking. That was the most useful article I had and the most valuable. It was the frying pan for omelettes, fritters and many other things; and lastly it was the roof of my pastry oven.

The latter I will describe—a circular hole in the ground about one foot in depth and the same in diameter. The fire required would be made near to the hole, and during the day all the spare embers would be gathered into it. In the evening, when the pastry was ready, the fire would be taken out and the pastry put in as follows:

First, a moderate-sized tart or fruit pie, above which a piece of tin -in general a preserved meat tin beat straight— resting on something on each side to keep it clear of the tart. On this would be placed two or three small tarts according to the quantity required, and above them all I placed the blade of the shovel on which more fire was laid.

When the wind was very high, of course, we had to put up with the numerous cinders which found their way into the oven and among the tarts. I must admit that the colour of my pastry sometimes was not exactly what it should have been to tempt a delicate stomach, but the quality of the tools must be taken into consideration.

My pastry board was the top of an old bottled-beer box and this was the only article I had to answer the purpose of a table, on which I used to clean my knives, boots, harness, etc. Consequently the pastry was at times somewhat of a dingy colour, yet many times have I heard my Master's guests say:

"I cannot imagine how it is your servant manages to turn out such excellent pastry. I will send my servant over to get a lesson from him."

But it was of no use for them to send their servants to me. I had not forgotten the lesson I got from one of them in the laundry line. However, I was persuaded by my Master to give some Little instruction to the Hottentot who assisted the servant of Captain Tench. This was the gentleman who gave my Master the starch, and if the Hottentot only carried out the instructions I gave him in the manner I intended, I feel perfectly satisfied I had my revenge for the starch business.

Within a short distance of our Camp there was a very fine stream of water, but we had been in the Camp for some time without making the discovery that the stream abounded in fish.It was made by an Irishman,and a very particular friend of mine with whom I had been on several excursions for various purposes, and moreover, Paddy was considered the best angler in the Regiment.

I procured some tackle belonging to my Master and lent it to Paddy on the understanding that he should give me a portion of the fish he caught, which he did. And as my Master was dining out that evening I cooked them for myself.

Paddy was most particular in his instructions to me not to tell anyone of the discovery he had made. "Doan't wishper a wurd about it," said he, but before 24 hours had passed everyone in the Camp knew of it. The following day me and Paddy went together. In the meantime he had succeeded in manufacturing a second line.

On reaching the stream there were several scattered along the bank, catching fish very fast. Soon I was as busy as the rest. Presently I heard some high words passing between my chum and another man near him who was complaining of Paddy throwing his line so close to his.

Who the stranger was I could not imagine. He wore a portion of the uniform of the "Old Ninety Ones," yet there was something about him that did not correspond exactly with the usual style of that did distinguished Regiment. I could hear they were getting at warm words, something like the following:

Paddy: "What are yez growling about? Shure an' yez want a mighty dale o' room."

Stranger: "Whether I want little or much is my business. I was here first and have a right to the place, and I think you have a good cheek to throw your line in so close to mine. Go a little further if you please."

Paddy: "Here fust, was yer? How cud yez be here first? I was here yesterday. Get out o' dat yer omadhon."

At this moment I was busy unhooking a very fine fish and preparing my line, and more words had passed between Paddy and the stranger of which I had not taken any particular notice of. I certainly had heard a bit of a scuffle, but was too much occupied at the time that several minutes elapsed before I looked around to show Paddy the fine fish I had caught, and I saw him standing with one hand to his nose and looking rather out of sorts.

"Why, Paddy," said I, "your nose is bleeding."

"Faith, I know it," said he. "And when I get howld of that feller I'll give him summut for himself."

I could also see that Paddy had got a black eye and his line lay on the ground in pieces. The stranger had walked away toward the Camp while Paddy vowed "vingeance agin the murthering vilyan," and eventually disappeared among the tents at the Officers' end of the Camp.

Paddy was about to follow him, but as I knew he was no great hand at the pugilistic art I advised him to let the matter drop and Paddy had the good sense not to tell anyone how he came by the black eye. When the men were doing up the horses in the evening one of the Officers noticed that Paddy had a black eye and asked the Troop Sergeant Major to enquire how Paddy had got it.

"How did you get that black eye, O'Neil?"

Paddy looked very sheepish when he replied:

"Faith, I had a fall over one of the tent ropes this afternoon; that's the way I got it."

But the Officer appeared to have his doubts about the truth of it as he asked Paddy if anyone saw him fall as stated. However, there was nothing more about it.

My Master did not speak in very high terms of the fish dinner I gave him. I believe myself it was rather rough. In the evening I was ordered to get out a bottle of sherry and two tin tots. Very few of the Officers in Camp could boast of having glasses to drink out of. Another Officer was in the hut with my Master whom I immediately recognized as the thrasher of my chum Paddy, and the very best fighting Officer in the 91st Regiment.

Chapter Twenty-One

Lost

As the Camp was about to be divided into two Divisions, Sir George Berkeley, the General in Command, invited all the Officers to dine with him. A message was sent round the camp by Sir Harry Darell, of the 7th Dragoon Guards, requesting all men who could sing a song or give a recitation to assemble at the General's marquee at 8 p.m.

It is scarcely necessary for me to say I was one of the party. We, the singers, took up our position under the fly or side of the tent. After a few songs had been sung a can of grog was handed out and a small tot, and we were told to help ourselves. Some of the party did so somewhat too freely.

About 11 p.m., whether from excitement or the strength of the grog I cannot say, but about that time several of the singers were entirely unable to give even one verse of a song. The finale was called for. Such an attempt at the National Anthem I never heard before or since, and the singers, except myself, staggered off to their tents.

I was asked by Sir Harry Darell to sit inside the marquee, where I sang several songs with which the General expressed himself highly pleased and sent wine to me several times. My last song—a new one, "*Paddy Among the Kaffirs*"—caused great laughter. I was asked to sing it again, which I did, and several glasses of wine were offered me.

The party broke up about 1 a.m. and up to this time I can safely say I thought myself perfectly sober, but when I reached my little held tent I found I was not. My Master called me to pull off his boots. I would much rather have stayed where I was. However, I answered the call. When I stooped to take hold of his boot I tumbled head foremost to the ground.

"Halloa, Adams," said he. "What is the matter with you? Why, you look to me as if you were not sober. Go away to your tent. I will manage to pull the boots off myself."

"No, Sir," said I, sitting on the ground, "let me pull them off," and I seized hold of the boot, saying, "I can't fall far now, Sir."

I gave a pull and my Master came head-first over me. To render any assistance was quite out of my power, so I made my way to my tent. My Master called me several times, but it was no use. He was quite right; I was not sober. Neither was he.

The following day the Camp was divided into two Divisions. One was sent to King William's Town and the other to Fort White. My Master and I went to the latter, which was only a short distance.

On our arrival, after pitching my Master's tent, I began to unpack my traps when I made the discovery that while I had been out singing the previous night someone had stolen my *sine quâ non*, the blade of the shovel. This loss completely ruined me. I suspected a brother flunkey, the fellow who gave me the lesson in the laundry line. I told my Master of the loss although the article in question was my property, also the fellow I suspected as being the thief.

He said: "Never mind, Adams. It is a bad job. You must do the best you can without it."

I made up my mind if I ever came across the fellow I suspected, I would have a good look among his traps, and if I found the shovel he might look out.

November 30th, 1847. A Kaffir came into Camp this morning with five goats and wanted to sell therm. My Master was away from Camp at the time in command of a Patrol Party. Had he been present I felt satisfied he would have bought them as he was very fond of goat's milk in his coffee, which he could drink every hour in the day.

After a little consideration I made up my mind to become the purchaser. I gave an old pair of overalls of my Master's, a stick of tobacco, one penny and three brass buttons, and the Kaffir appeared well satisfied.

When my Master returned he was much pleased at me buying the goats and offered me ten shillings to make them over to him to which I consented.And within one hour it would be impossible to tell the number of his friends he had promised should have a little milk for their evening cup. I had also engaged a little Kaffir boy to take them out to graze during the day and bring them back at sunset.

About the third day after my purchase my Master had dined—that is,if one might call a glass of sherry and a biscuit a dinner. He could not possibly make a dinner off what I had prepared for him that day; namely, a piece of half-boiled beef, tough as leather, no vegetables, a little soup and that more like dirty water. It was utterly impossible to cook anything; the rain had put my fire out several times that day. He was anxiously waiting for his coffee, and several servants were there also with their little pots waiting for the promised luxury, but the goats had not arrived. At length my Master got impatient and said:

"Now, Adams, let me have my coffee, please. Don't put quite so much milk as you did last night but a little more coffee."

I felt sorry the goats had not arrived as I knew my Master had made no dinner. At length I was obliged to tell him he would have to take his coffee without milk this evening as the goats had not come in.

His temper was up in one moment.

"Why, you must be a fool to trust the goats to that boy. I knew how it would be. You won't see them any more."

"Can't help it," said I. "Must do as we have done before— do without."

I waited some little time and, finding they did not return, I went in search of them.After a time I fancied I saw them grazing on the side of a hill.I made my way toward the spot, and when I reached it there was no goats there.

I kept my eyes, as I thought, on the exact position of the Camp, and continued my search. At length it began to get dark and I thought I had better return to the Camp. I walked a considerable distance, in fact much farther than I fancied I had, when searching for the goats. Still no Camp came in sight.

Darkness set in and with it a heavy rain. I began to feel anything but comfortable. The time had passed for the cattle to be returning to the Camp from grazing and I had not heard the cracking of any of the drivers' whips. In vain I listened; there was not the slightest sound to be heard. The darkness was most intense, not a star to be seen. One minute I would think, "It's no use standing still," and the next "If I moved I might go further from the Camp."

At last I got into the branches of a tree. I was not afraid of wolves or jackalls although I knew they were pretty numerous about there, but I did not know whether a stray Lion might be roaring about and take a fancy to me. Two or three times I heard the report of a gun, but too far off to tell from what direction the sound came. Once I fancied I heard the sound of a bugle or trumpet.

I remained in the tree until daylight, when I again started in search of the Camp. The only thing I was afraid of—in fact, dreaded—was falling into the hands of the Kaffirs. No white man ever received any mercy from them. The sun was pretty high and I began to feel faint. If I could only find a tree sufficiently high that would enable me to see over the top of the ordinary bush, I should be able to see the smoke rising from the position of the Camp, but there was no such tree to be found.

At length I came to a kind of road on which were the marks of horses' feet. The toes of the shoes pointed both ways—as many one way as the other. At length I fixed on the way I would take, and had not proceeded far when I heard the sound of a bugle I shouted with all my might. It proved to be three of the Cape Mounted Rifles. They were one of several parties that had been sent out to search for me. I had wandered nearly seven miles from the Camp.

My Master was pleased when he saw me, and said he hoped it would be a caution to me in future. The goats had returned that morning. The boy said he had lost his way in the bush and could not find the Camp. I believe he told the truth as the goats had not been milked.

December 5th, 1847. An Officer who had recently arrived from England dined with my Master who had exchanged from some Regiment to the Cape Mounted Rifles. He told my Master in my presence that he was not going to stay in the Cape mounted Rifles; he had no liking for Hottentots and he did not want to go beyond civilization altogether, in fact that he was already negotiating for another exchange, this time into the 7th Dragoon Guards.

I think beyond a doubt he was the most comical Officer I ever met in the Service. His name was Captain A. C. Bentinck. He did join the 7th and eventually became Colonel of the Regiment. The present Duke of Portland was born during the Colonelcy of his father.

The Kaffir from whom I bought the goats came into the Camp with a horse for sale. It was only a common hack and he only wanted what I could afford to give for it, and I thought it would answer very well for a hack pack horse for the field. My Master was away from the Camp at the time, and I did not feel disposed to be in a hurry about buying it; and, another thing, I was not sufficiently master of the Kaffir language to closely question him as to where he got the horse from.

At length a Hottentot friend of mine came up who was well up in the Kaffir language and, the Kaffir's answers being satisfactory, I bought the horse. My Master returned shortly after and I heard his voice:

"Here, Adams, drive this strange horse away; he is eating all Pompey's forage."

I told him I had bought the horse and given 14 sticks of

tobacco. an old knife and all the brass buttons I could find for him. I thought he would answer very well for a hack during the time we remained in the field.

But my Master was not of the same opinion. He said:

"Can't you see that horse is a great deal too good to have been long in the hands of a Kaffir? Besides, he is shod."

I never thought to look at that or I should have known directly that he had been stolen. However, my Master told me that he was going to King William's Town that evening and that I was to go with him. and advised me to take the new bought horse with me as he had no doubt but we should find the owner of him. I had made up my mind, if he was not claimed, to sell him. I did not intend to bring him back to the camp.

We reached King William's Town the following morning. I was busy feeding the horses—two of my Master's and I bought—when an Officer belonging to the Engineers came up and asked me if the horse was mine.

" Yes," said I. "Will you buy him?"

The Officer had another look at him, when he said:

"You say that horse is yours. Just let me tell you, that horse is mine. He was stolen from me five days ago, and I shall claim him and give you in charge of the Provost Marshal for having the horse in your possession. Who are you?"

I told him I was a Dragoon and servant to an Officer in the 7th Dragoon Guards. Lucky for me, my Master came up before I fell into the hands of the Provost Marshal. They had a few minutes conversation, during which I heard my Master say: "Honest as the day, but a perfect fool." I cannot say I was exactly of the same opinion.

The Officer took possession of the horse and gave me a sovereign. I suppose that was for my stupidity, and advised me to be more careful the next horse I bought or I might not get off quite so well.

Chapter Twenty-Two
Kychee

December 8th, 1847. Started on a three days' patrol—Artillery 2 guns, 20 Dragoons and 50 Infantry—into the Amatola to destroy huts and crops. The Kaffirs were creeping back. They were getting tired of war. Their ammunition was getting low. We took no tents with us. Each man was served out with 11/2 lbs. of biscuits—at the rate of 8 oz. per day—and we were to trust to the Kaffirs for meat. Each man received 150 rounds of ammunition.

The first two nights the Kaffirs fired a few shots at our bivouac, but done us no harm. On the morning of the third day we were making our way back to Camp. Up to that time we had not seen a Kaffir, the three days we had been out, when we came in sight of a very large *Kraal* containing about 20 very poor cattle. These were the first we had seen, with the exception of one or two strays which had been shot to furnish us with meat.

There was about 30 huts, all newly built, but not a Kaffir to be seen. We took possession of the cattle and drove them before us until we had reached within three miles of the Camp without meeting a single Kaffir, when one made his appearance as a "Flag of Truce," his body being covered with white clay. We were just entering a thick, bushy ravine.

The Kaffir wanted us to give them back the cattle we had taken. That was not at all likely. He was allowed to go back again, and a few minutes after, just as we were in the most dense part of the ravine, the Kaffirs opened fire.

It was a good job for us they had such faith in their guns. Had they attacked us on the plain with the assegaie and the same amount of pluck they showed in the bush, they would have given us something to have done to keep possession of the cattle. Twice the Kaffirs rushed among the Troops and endeavoured to call the cattle away from us. They strove their hardest, but it was no use. They were bayonetted by the Infantry in numbers. The slaughter was horrible.

One fellow seized hold of the reins of the pack horse I was leading. He paid very dearly for it. I let go the reins for a moment only, drew my sword and drove it through his body. Since the time when the saddle bags turned round under the horse's belly, I had never gone without my sword and a pistol belonging to my Master. The loss of the enemy must have been very great. We had only five wounded.

December 12, 1847. A son of Chief Maccomo came into the Camp to sue for peace for his father. It was with his Tribe that we had the skirmish on the 10th inst. The young Chief was a very intelligent fellow. He had but recently returned from England, where he had been sent by the Government to be educated. He had been 7 years in England. He was at this time I should think, about 22 years of age, and, with the exception of a magnificent *kaross* which was partly folded over the right shoulder he was perfectly naked the same as the rest of the Tribe.

I had the pleasure of a few minutes' conversation with him. It did not seem natural to hear a fine looking young fellow, a Kaffir, speaking good English, with a thick rope of very common beads round his neck and a feather stuck in each of his ears. Although he was sueing for peace, he did not hesitate to say that the Kaffirs were fully justified in all they had done. England had no more right to their country than they had to take England. It was merely a question of might against right.

He had a long interview with the General, who told him that the money which had been paid by England for his education had been thrown away, and also informed him that he must leave the Camp at sunset. The young Chief expressed a wish to remain in the Camp for a few days, (but was told that this) would not be allowed and was further told if he was found in the Camp after that time he would be treated as a prisoner and very probably shot. This information surprised him so much that he left the Camp at once.

December 13th, 1847. A number of Kaffir women came into Camp to sue for peace. Among them was the wife of a Chief whose name was, I believe, Seyola.

This woman was the granddaughter of General Campbell, who, with his three daughters, was wrecked off the Coast but succeeded in reaching the shore, when they were made prisoners by the Kaffirs. The youngest daughter became the wife of a Chief and had several children of which only one survived, who eventually became the wife of Seyola, the present Chief. Her name was Nunnoobee, but she was sometimes called Nebudoo. Miss Campbell, other mother, had been dead some years. It was not known what had become of the General and his two eldest daughters. One of them was reported to have become the wife of Umtikaka, another Chief, but I believe this was never authenticated. Nunnoobee appeared about 30 years of age and quite evidently of European blood. Her hair was long and matted and her whole appearance was filthy in the extreme.

The same day there was quite a lark in the Camp. A young Kaffir girl made her way into the tent of the General's Aide de Camp during his absence and the lady prepared to take up her quarters for an indefinite period. When the owner of the tent returned he had some considerable difficulty in persuading her to vacate his quarters. She said she was willing to do anything for him, even become his wife, if he would only give them peace. At sunset, much to their surprise, they were all turned out of Camp.

December 14th, 1847. A report reached the Camp that there were many thousand women and children concealed in the Amatola Mountains and great numbers of them were dying of starvation. A detachment was ordered off at once on patrol. We kept on the move all day, but saw no Kaffirs, male or female.

At sunset there was a heavy thunderstorm. We had no tents and were not allowed to make any fires. The rain continued throughout the night. You may believe me when I say that standing still in a heavy rain for 10 hours, holding two horses, is anything but a pleasant occupation. The rain did not cease until some time after sunrise, when, after the usual bush breakfast, we moved on again.

At midday we came to a Kraal which contained about 60 fine cattle and about 30 goats, which we took possession of, after which the Kraal and the whole of the huts were set fire to. The Kaffirs had cleared off into the bush. We drove the cattle a short distance when we halted for refreshment. One bullock and two or three goats were killed, after which we settled down for the night. And such a one I never passed, the Kaffirs blazing away the whole of the night. The shots whistled over our heads among the bush like hailstones. At daylight we had four wounded, had lost nearly half the cattle and goats. It was surprising to all that we managed to keep any of the cattle, as it was a well-known fact that all cattle reared in Kaffirland will follow the voice of a Kaffir anywhere. They said "The cattle knew who were their best friends. We would keep and feed them well, but you people would kill them."

I heard that two of the wounded had died before we reached the Camp. That was not of much consequence; material to be shot at was cheap.

December 18th, 1847. I began to find the work more than I could manage. My Master wanted his coffee at 4 a.m., and from that time until 11 p.m. I had but little rest. He was quite willing to pay for any assistance if I could get it, but I could not get any as my Master would not give brandy in addition or in lieu of payment – which was quite right because, should the man be reported drunk he would say, most likely "I had no drink only what Captain So-an-so gave me," and the Officer would be severely reprimanded. I don't say that every man would make that excuse, but there were a great many that would.

My Master was exceedingly kind and most liberal, but he wanted a great deal of attention and waiting upon. I had four horses to look after; and no one that has not had experience in such work in Camp can have the most remote idea of the amount of labour there is attached to such a job, particularly in wet weather, when the horses are restless and continually rolling in the mud. Many times when I have been so busy I did not know what to do first, he has called me for the most trifling purpose, perhaps to fill his pipe or interpret something that one of the Hottentots might be talking about. When he called, I would answer him and no more. Sometimes he would come to me and say, "Adams, I want you to splice another piece on my pipe," and I invariably made him this reply:

"If the pipe is of more consequence than the horses, I will do it, but if not, you must mend the pipe yourself."

After which he would walk away and sulk for the remainder of the day.

In the evening when I had everything prepared for his dinner and wished to know when he would be ready for it, he would annoy me by saying he was going to dine with some other Officer but would take coffee when he returned - at which time he invariably found there was none ready for him and would have to wait until I lit the fire and made it. Then when I took it into his hut, he would pretend to be fast asleep.

Once or twice in this book I have mentioned the name of Kychee- a name that had been associated with mine for the past sixteen months. She was a Hottentot, and when I think of all the troubles and hardships she went through for my sake, the many sacrifices she made for my comfort, I am sure she is not unworthy of at least one page in my diary on which to record some little acknowledgment of her devotion.

It was after I first came out of the Hospital at Fort Peddie that I met the Hottentot lady in question. She was then servant to the Commissioner's lady and was in the habit of walking out with the children. She accompanied me to Cawood's Post and afterwards to Fort Beaufort. Had it not been for her on that road, I must have starved and rotted. While I remained in Hospital Kychee went into service with Mrs. Beaver, wife of the Chaplain, and when I came out again she joined me and followed the Army which took the field in December, 1846.

Shall I ever forget Christmas Day of that year! We had not a morsel of food, yet there was not a murmur out of poor Kychee. During the night she came to me with a piece of Dutch bread which she had begged from one of the waggon drivers, and well do I remember the trouble I had to prevail on her to take only a small portion of it.

Being an Officer's servant some portion of the time, I had many opportunities of getting food, which otherwise I should not have had, still we were often on exceedingly short commons. At such times her schemes and contrivances for making excuses for not eating her share of the little we had would fill a volume. Sometimes she would feign sickness in order that I might be induced to eat more than my share. If she succeeded her eyes would sparkle with delight.

While on that expedition I lost her for five days. I found out afterwards that she dare not enter Kreli's country as they made slaves of all Hottentots found in their territory. She was obliged to hide herself in the bush, and had nothing to subsist upon except what roots she could find and a small piece of tobacco which I had given her as her daily allowance when I left her. She knew that we were bound to come back the same way. In conclusion I shall say that a more faithful, devoted creature never existed than the poor little Hottentot, Kychee.

Chapter Twenty Three
The Arrival of Sir Harry Smith

December 25th, 1847. Christmas Day and all the Troops were on short rations. It rained all day - the Camp was knee deep in mud - and in striving to cook my Master's dinner I was nearly blinded with the smoke. Several times the rain put out my fire entirely. At such times I was not the most amiable person one could wish to see, and well my Master knew it. Still, he must have been good-tempered sometimes or he would certainly have cried out this evening when I put his dinner on the table. I hope I shall be pardoned for calling it such a name.

"Adams," said he, "this is a horrid mess. True, I am hungry, but I cannot eat raw meat."

I did not know what to say. I certainly felt disgusted. At length I said:

"It's no use grumbling. I can't help it. The rain put my fire out the moment I left it, and the horses must be attended to, particularly in such weather as this."

He replied: "Quite right, Adams. Never mind the dinner. Give me a biscuit and a tot of sherry and water, and just fill my pipe for me."

My Master was particularly fond of the "weed" and was always in a passable mood when blowing a cloud. Having got the steam up, he called me in and said:

"Adams, this is Christmas Day and no dinner."

"I am very sorry," said I, "but the rain put my fire out so many times and the horses were so restless."

"Well, never mind. Take a few biscuits and some cheese, and here is some brandy you can share with your comrade. But bear in mind I shall not want you to pull off my boots this evening."

I was in hopes he had forgotten that little mistake of mine.

However, I sent for my chum and shared with him my Christmas dinner after which we had a pipe and some pleasant chat about our friends at home - "Home, that magic sound of sweetest of words which brings to the mind of the exiled soldier visions of the days of his youth" - and to the best of my recollection we got somewhat sentimental. But about 10 o'clock several shots were fired, and in less than five minutes the whole Camp was under arms.

The cause was soon ascertained. During the past four nights several cattle had been stolen from the Commissariat Kraal, and the Guard in charge could give no account of them. The fact was, these Dutch Burghers were very bad ones for night duty. They could not be prevented from sleeping on their post. This night they had been changed and a number of Hottentots put on watch inside the Kraal.

Three Kaffirs had been seen twice during the night by the watchful Totties, but these Kaffirs were not interfered with. The third time they came after a good look round they entered the Kraal, and were allowed to select their booty and were in the act of driving them off when the Hottentots fired at them and shot all three of them. Two of them were recognized as having been employed as herds by the Commissariat, and the third as the notorious Cobus Congo, a half-breed Kaffir and one of the greatest marauders in all Kaffirland. He had been a prisoner several times but had always managed to escape punishment, but this time had settled his career.

December 27th, 1847. My Master obtained for me ten days' leave of absence to accompany the Patrol which left the Camp every third day for the purpose of conveying dispatches to and from the Colony. I was to proceed to Fort Beaufort to ascertain if any supplies had reached the Frontiers, as my Master had been expecting some from England for some time past. I also had some little business to transact for myself. I wished to get married to a Dutch girl.

There was no mistake about the young lady being genuine, both in speech and build. She could not speak one word of English, and I should think her weight - asking pardon for mentioning such a thing in reference to a lady - could not have been less than 16 stone. Her age, 14.

On reaching the Fort, I first ascertained that no stores had reached there for my Master. I then hastened to visit my lady love and asked her in marriage, as I had an idea of settling in the country on the Frontiers. But the mama of the young lady declined to give her consent on account of her daughter's youth, but promised her consent when the war was over, providing I was not killed and several other provisos too numerous to mention. I remained with them three days. I was able to converse with them in their own language.

In fact I may here mention that I have been in all four quarters of the Globe. I was never in any place twelve months except one, that I did not learn the language pretty well in that time. The one place which beat me was Ireland. I never could get properly hold of the brogue, the full extent of my knowledge of which was only a few words such as "*A turrum pogue a colleen hogue*" which I believe means, "Give me a kiss, my pretty girl."

My time of leave having expired, I bid my lady love and prospective mother-in-law goodbye. I have no doubt had I pressed the old lady she would have given her consent. However, I never saw them again. About this time Sir Harry Smith arrived on the Frontiers and hostilities were suspended.

When I arrived at Fort Hare with the Patrol party, I was informed that the next party would not leave the Fort for two hours, but before one hour had elapsed the party had gone on and I was left behind. However anxious I might have been to get back, I did not feel disposed to risk the journey by myself, consequently I was obliged to wait for the following party. I took good care not to miss that one.

When I reached Fort White I was three days behind my time and my Master was as savage as a bear. He said he had been living on biscuits for the past week and the horses were sick for the want of cleaning. I was rather pleased that he missed me - "fool" as he thought me.

January 16th, 1848. Nearly a waggonload of supplies reached the Camp for my Master, consisting of preserved meat, fish, fowl and vegetables, with wine and bottled beer. When he came to examine the list he found that one-third of his stores had, as he said, "evaporated." However, he was quite delighted.

"Now, Adams," said he, "I am going to have three friends to dine with me this evening. If you can manage it for us, let us have something very nice. You can take anything you want from the stock, but let us have a dinner for once in a while."

I got the servants of the invited guests to assist me, who each brought their cooking utensils, which was a great assistance to me, particularly since I had lost my shovel-blade. Each servant brought his Master's camp stool, tin pot, tin plate, knife, fork and spoon.

At length the dinner hour arrived. My Master had been to the fire several times under the pretence of getting a light to his pipe but in reality to see how the dinner was progressing, and in order that everything might go on all right he had given two men a tot of brandy each to water and feed the horses.

The soup was pronounced "superb," fish "really beautiful," potted woodcock "magnificent," joint and vegetables superior to anything they had seen for months past," and one of them told my Master that he had the best field cook in all Kaffirland, to which encomium my Master did not reply. But the pastry, although not of a very good colour, "surpassed all."

When they had settled down to their wine, we - that is, the cook and his assistants - received each a bottle of beer, with a bottle of brandy between the whole. The time passed merrily in the "kitchen"; and I might say the same of the "hall," if allowed to form an opinion by the boisterous singing of "He's A Jolly Good Fellow."

About midnight coffee was called for, and shortly after all was quiet. Coffee was much earlier in requisition the following morning than usual.

January 17th, 1848. Peace was proclaimed throughout all Kaffirland. In reference to which, what was the general opinion? Was it creditable to England? I am of opinion that it was not. Sir Harry Smith had had some little experience with the Kaffirs in a former war - I believe in 1834 and 1835- and was under the impression that the same tactics would answer in 1848. But the Kaffir of the former period was not to be compared with the latter, any more than those of 1848 are to be compared with the Zulus of the present day. I think everyone will admit that to be correct.

When Sir Harry Smith arrived at the Frontiers he had two articles made; namely, a wooden sword and a long staff with a ball at the end. Each of those were carried by one of his Escort, and when marching up the country the Kaffirs came to meet Sir Harry Smith at the different Camps or Forts, but none of them with arms, the two wooden articles were offered to the Kaffirs. If they chose war they were to touch the sword. If they wanted peace, they were to touch the staff.

All this was looked upon as a complete farce. As a matter of course, they all wanted peace. They had had enough of war for the present; in fact were being thoroughly beaten in detail by want of ammunition and starvation. "Yes," they said, "they would do anything that their father-Sir Harry Smith-told them." And thus ended the war which had lasted one year and eleven months, and all over an old chopper worth fourpence.

I wonder if I should be considered inquisitive if I were to ask what became of the amounts deducted from the soldier, monthly, during that war for rations he never received? The following statement was submitted at different times to those in authority and, although it was never disputed, the amount was never allowed. I put the average strength of the Army during the war at 5,000 men. Each man lost about 125 rations, which at five pence per ration would amount to £2.12.1, the whole sum amounting to £13,020.16.8.

Where did that money go? Who reaped the benefit of it? Not the soldier, he was basely robbed of it. By whom? That is a question I have never been able to get answered.

January 20th, 1848. My Regiment was ordered to England and a General Order was issued to the effect that any man might leave the Regiment with a free discharge, no matter how short his service had been (if he wished) to remain in the Colony. If they desired to become agriculturists they would get implements and seed free of cost, and so many acres of land. A great many availed themselves of this most excellent offer.

I gave in my name to remain in the Colony, as I had the offer of a good situation as storekeeper to a man who was in a very extensive way of business. His name was Webster and he was the father of the young man I met with in Griqua Town in 1845. I was well qualified for the situation as I could speak Dutch as fluently as I could English, but I was so foolish as to listen to the promises of my Master that I withdrew my name from the list, and thereby threw away the best chance I ever had in my life.

A few days afterwards the Regiment received the order to march down the country and my Master desired me to unpack the whole of his stores and lay them out separately in front of his hut, as he intended giving them away among the Officers in the Camp. He told me I could take a few things for myself, which I did pretty freely – fortunate for him I did so or he would have gone very short when on the road afterwards. In fact he was so elated at the thought of returning to England that I really wondered he did not give his bed away.

January 22nd, 1848. We began our march toward England, and I should think we were about the most comical lot of soldiers as Dragoons that ever were seen in Her Majesty's

Service. Our uniform, like Joseph's coat, was of many colours; all more or less patched with pieces of sheep or buckskin.Our headgear was equally of as great a variety from the regimental forage cap to the red or blue nightcap, and one or two black pots were slung to every saddle. But with regard to the men, the few men that were left, something after the same stamp as myself, were as dark-skinned as the Kaffirs and hardy enough to go through another two years war.

What had become of all the boasters of five years ago? The heavy Dragoons, they were either dead or discharged. I have said before and I still maintain it - for thorough hard work in Camp or Quarters, peace or war, there are none who can beat the men of 10 stone weight.As I have began to speak of five years ago, it is quite evident that I am getting near the end of this book.A few more incidents and I shall have done.

Our first march "homeward" was completed, and as my Master had given away all his stores as far as he knew, I thought I would wait and see what he was going to do about food. I had put up his tent and made him some coffee when he asked me what I was going to do about dinner. I said:

"You gave away all your things in the Camp, so I don't know what you are going to do between here and Fort Beaufort."

He replied:"Oh, never mind. Must put up with a biscuit for a day or two."

But I let him know he had not given all away by putting him up a very good dinner, which I think was quite enough to convince him I was not quite such a fool as he thought I was. If I had been, he would have had to go a good many days on biscuits.

Chapter Twenty Four
Embarking Again

At length we reached Graham's Town. The best horses of the Regiment were selected for the Cape Mounted Rifles and the remainder were sold by public auction. My Master's horses did not realize one half of their value.

Here I again requested to leave him as I wished to remain in the Colony. He begged me to remain with him until we reached Algoa Bay, when he would pay my expenses back to the Frontier and would make me a handsome present besides and I foolishly consented, and on the following day a General Order was published to the effect that no further applications for free discharge were to be sent in. Thus I lost an opportunity which never occurred again, and there was a great change in my Master in his manner toward me from that day.

The Regiment had by this time for various reasons been reduced to about 100 men. Now we had to finish the journey to Algoa Bay or Port Elizabeth on foot.

On reaching there, my Master put up at the Phoenix Hotel, and as his wardrobe required some little additions before he could make any kind of a decent appearance, I was instructed to go to town with the following orders:

1st. Take the large portmanteau and get it repaired.

2nd. Find a tailor and send him up to the Hotel with a lot of clothes, pretty good but not the best.

3rd. Find a bootmaker, good one, and tell him to bring up a lot of boots.

4th. Send up a hosier with shirts, drawers, socks, etc.

5th. A hatter with a number of hats.

6th. A respectable barber, as he wanted a bushel of hair taken off his head and face.

7th. And lastly, go to a house described by my Master as being about three miles from the town, and buy a large monkey he had seen marked "For Sale," and gave me two pounds for the purpose.

He said he did not think it was more than three miles, but I was to be sure and get the monkey. In short, not to return without it.

Already that morning I had walked 15 miles and now had, with this number of orders to attend to, at least 10 miles further to walk.

However, I started, and managed to execute all the orders with the exception of the one in reference to the monkey, and as I had not had anything to eat since I left the Camp at 5 a.m. and had marched 15 miles, I felt somewhat hungry and began to look about for some place that would furnish the needful.

I was on the point of giving that up as a hopeless case, when, on passing a small house the door of which stood open, I saw a man with his family at dinner. I stepped to the door and asked the man if he could let me have something to eat. I was willing to pay whatever he might charge.

"You are an Englishman," he said, "and such as I have, you are welcome to partake."

There were boiled fish, stewed pumpkin and bread, and any quantity of grapes and apricots. I made a hearty meal. When I asked what amount I had to pay, the man replied:

"I shall not charge you anything for the fish and fruit, but you have eaten a shilling's worth of bread. Why, you must have been nearly starved."

I admitted that I was very hungry. I gave him a shilling for the bread and another for a bottle of wine, which I begged him to accept. He would only do that on condition that I should stay and take one glass of it, after which I continued my journey in search of the monkey, and was actually thinking of giving up any further search when I met a Native Constable of whom I enquired. "Yes," he said, "there was a monkey for sale about a mile further along the road."

At length I found the monkey. He was owned by a Malay and the animal being a fine one, he wanted twenty-two shillings for him, collar and chain included, which amount I gave and the beast was handed over to me.

I shall never forget the trouble I had to get the brute along. He snapped and flew at everyone he came near, and when I attempted to check him by shaking his chain he flew at me and bit me on both legs and tore the lower part of my trousers to pieces. At length he became quite unmanageable and would not go the way I wanted him. To make things more unpleasant, about a dozen darkies gathered round me and began to laugh at me.

An old gentleman who was standing near began to give me some advice, saying a monkey would often go with a Native when they will not be led by a white man. I asked several who were standing near if they would take charge of him for me and I would pay them but not one of the niggers would have anything to do with him.

At this moment the old gentleman made a step forward- as I thought, to make much of the monkey - when the brute rushed forward to the full extent of his chain and seized the old chap by the leg, biting him severely and tore his trousers. At this the darkies set up a roar of laughter, in the midst of which a Constable came up. One of the niggers made a poke at the monkey with his stick. I expect that was to stir him up a bit. At all events it stirred me up as I immediately hit the darkie on the nose and down he went.

This brought things to a crisis. The old gentleman gave me and the monkey in charge, and we started off to the lock-up. But before we reached there the monkey had taken a piece out of the trousers of the Constable, who tried to knock him on the head with his staff, but Jacko was too smart for him.

At length we reached the lock-up and fortunately for me, the Officer was there or I should have been locked up until the next day. The Magistrate - a Police Officer - very soon settled my case by ordering me to pay five shillings to the old

210

gentleman as compensation, three shillings to the Constable, five shillings fine for the assault on the darkie and three shillings cost- and,lastly, had to give a Hottentot two shillings to carry the monkey to the Hotel.The brute went with the Totty as quiet as a lamb.

I found my Master in a sweet temper.The moment he saw me he began:"Did I think he was going to wear such clothes as I had sent him? The tailor told him I had selected them myself. They were fit only for a waggon driver. The bootmaker had brought boots fit only for a clodhopper. No hatter or hosier had been near him, and the smell of the barber had been enough to poison him."

"And where had I been the whole of the day? Where was the monkey? That was not the one he wanted.He would not have that brute as a gift."And my Master made an attempt to kick him when the monkey seized him by the leg and tore his trousers; and had it not been for the Hottentot who bore a striking resemblance to the monkey, my Master would have been severely bitten.

But when I told him my adventures and the costs amounting to £2 - exactly the amount he gave me - his rage got beyond his reason. He ordered me to take the monkey back and get the twenty-two shillings. I told him he might do that himself;I had had quite enough to do with the brute. He then asked the Hottentot to take him back,and promised to give him five shillings when he returned for his trouble.

The Totty accepted the offer and I fully explained to him that he was to take back the monkey and return here with the money, twenty-two shillings; but I could plainly see by the cunning twinkle in his eye that he would not return in a hurry after he had once left. I told this to my Master, but was shut up in a peremptory manner with the words,"You mind your own business." However, I was right; we never saw either monkey or the Totty again.

All these annoyances combined put my Master in such a temper that he made use of language that was not exactly becoming to an Officer and a gentleman. Me being called a "stupid fool" and an "ass" I thought nothing of as I had become used to those terms during the last four months, although it was only in his moments of extreme passion that he made use of those words. Two of his former servants, who must have been somewhat more sensitive than I was, had left his service the first time he conferred that not very distinguished title on them.

At length my Master, having got beyond "blessing my eyes and limbs," I, like the worm, turned and "let go the painter." He, in return, exercised his authority, by rushing off to the Guard and returning with the Sergeant. I was forthwith marched off to the Guard House, a prisoner.

The following morning my Master came to visit me at the Guard House and said he was very sorry that I had let my temper get the better of me. I was under the impression that the boot was on the other leg. I knew he would have given anything if he could only have taken me out of the Guard House again. But he had not that power, as once a man was made a prisoner in the Main Guard he could only be released by the Officer Commanding. He asked me if I was not sorry for what I had said, but I quickly told him I was not. I was perfectly satisfied that he dreaded going before the Commanding Officer a great deal more than I did. From the time he joined the Regiment he had not been able to keep one servant as long as I had been with him. And the reason of it was his temper and every Officer in the Regiment knew it.

In the course of the day I was taken before the Commanding Officer and my crime read, which, as it had been sent in by my Master when he was at the height of his passion, was not couched in the mildest terms. It was as follows: "Gross insubordination to Captain Bunbury."

My Master did not press the charge against me, thinking I would still continue to be his servant. My previous good character stood to me and I was released with a caution. I was asked if I would go back as servant, but I refused. The past four months had been quite enough for me and I returned to my duty in the Ranks.

In justice to my late Master, I am bound to say when he was not in those fits of temper he was most kind, generous and liberal to a fault. He was Captain of my Troop for some years after in which I was a Private, and never once took advantage of his position to annoy me in any way in revenge for leaving his service.

February 3rd, 1848. The Regiment embarked at Algoa Bay and arrived at Cape Town on the 5th. I thought it was the prettiest place I ever saw, but having been some years in the wildest parts of Kaffirland no doubt added somewhat to my fancy. The Town was apparently inhabited by people of all Nations. The streets were very long and particularly clean.

We occupied the Bombproof Barracks built by the Dutch just beside the foot of Table Mountain. One portion of the Barracks was fitted up as a Theatre and was in possession, by permission of the authorities, of an Italian Theatrical Company.

At the recommendation of Sir Harry Darell, I was invited to join them, which I did. An agreement was entered into. I was to sing three nights two songs each night, for which I was to receive one pound. I got on remarkably well during the week, but could not get any money, but was promised five shillings extra if I would continue the engagement for another week. To this also I consented.

When I asked the following Saturday for a settlement of my claim -£2.5.0- I was informed by the Treasurer that all salaries would be paid at 10 a.m. the following Monday. At that time I waited with about 20 others for some considerable time. No one came to the office, and in the end we discovered that the Company had bolted and paid nobody.

While here I wrote some verses entitled *"Past Events in Kaffirland."* The copyright I sold to the Editor of The Cape

Town *Sam Slick* for five pounds and fifty copies. The latter I distributed among my friends.

March, 1848. I was present at the wedding of my old friend, "Susan." He married the daughter of a Corporal in the Regiment. For some time past he had been acting Deputy Assistant Schoolmaster - a berth that suited him far better than soldiering.

This brings me to the conclusion of my first five years in the Army.

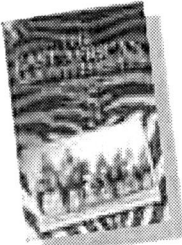

Printed in the United Kingdom by
Lightning Source UK Ltd., Milton Keynes
136539UK00001B/93/A